Withdrawn

3 9082 11771 6145

P9-DNC-422

WHY DIDN'T

I THINK

of

THAT?

WHY DIDN'T
I THINK

 *of*

THAT?

101 INVENTIONS THAT CHANGED
THE WORLD **BY HARDLY TRYING**

Anthony Rubino, Jr.

A adams media

AVON, MASSACHUSETTS

Published by
Adams Media, a division of F+W Media, Inc.
57 Littlefield Street, Avon, MA 02322. U.S.A.
www.adamsmedia.com

ISBN 10: 1-4405-0010-X
ISBN 13: 978-1-4405-0010-7

Printed in China

10 9 8 7 6 5 4 3 2 1

Library of Congress Cataloging-in-Publication Data
is available from the publisher.

This publication is designed to provide accurate and authoritative information with regard to the subject matter covered. It is sold with the understanding that the publisher is not engaged in rendering legal, accounting, or other
professional advice. If legal advice or other expert assistance is required, the
services of a competent professional person should be sought.
—From a *Declaration of Principles* jointly adopted by a Committee of the
American Bar Association and a Committee of Publishers and Associations

Many of the designations used by manufacturers and sellers to distinguish
their product are claimed as trademarks. Where those designations appear
in this book and Adams Media was aware of a trademark claim, the designations have been printed with initial capital letters.

This book is available at quantity discounts for bulk purchases.
For information, please call 1-800-289-0963.

To Luke, Jake, and Grace (in order of appearance).

Special thanks to the men and women whose humble master-pieces adorn the following pages.

Thanks to Mollye Miller for her hard work, dedication, and abundant talent.

Thanks also to Brendan O'Neill and Elisabeth Lariviere.

"Build a better mousetrap, and the world will beat a path to your door."—Ralph Waldo Emerson

C CONTENTS

INTRODUCTION

The Light Bulb
The Automobile
The Theory of Relativity
The Steam Engine
The Computer

What do all of these revolutionary inventions have in common?

None of them are in this book.

Why? Because the average person can't invent stuff like that, and this is an "invention book" for the average person.

I have compiled the stories behind 101 of the most extraordinarily simple inventions that have changed our world. In fact, in most cases, the astounding inventions described here required no special skills, no education, no expensive laboratories, no government grants, very little capital, just an extraordinary amount of hard work and ingenuity. This book is meant to inspire you, make you laugh a little (I hope), and encourage you through example to follow your dreams.

However, just because they're identified as simple, doesn't mean the inventors are simple-minded. Every one of these inventions is elegant—meaning, they all have refinement, grace, and beauty. The people who invented and discovered these things deserve to be recognized and praised.

All that said, you will see that there are inventions and discoveries listed here that would be impossible for you to have created, as their inceptions occurred long before you were born. Fire, the wheel, even golf—these are all amazingly simple but, now, out of your creative reach. Inventions and discoveries such as these are rendered here to display how, throughout history, ordinary people did extraordinary things time and time again.

But you will also find an astonishing array of modern items that you really *could* have invented had you been the first to think of them.

So turn the page, read on, and as you do, keep asking yourself, "Hey . . . *why didn't* I *think of that?*"

In the 1990s,
Post-It Notes
sales reached
$15,000,000,000.

1 POST-IT NOTES

TAGLINE: A scrap of paper and some glue

PREDECESSOR: A scrap of paper and some tape

LESSON: The solution to *your* problem might be the solution to *everybody's* problem.

It's the summer of 1974 . . . you're begging Rikki not to lose that number, wondering what flavor lollipop is Kojak's favorite, and just spent $3.50 on a Pet Rock (page 53).

Meanwhile, 3M employee Art Fry is trying to figure out how to prevent his bookmark from falling out of his hymnal during choir practice. His colleague, Dr. Spencer Silver, just developed a new adhesive that's sticky, but not too sticky. It allows users to fasten things without leaving behind residue, making it possible to reposition once-stuck things. A problem-and-solution match made in inventor's heaven.

Fry used Silver's glue to develop a solution to his problem. Soon he was belting out "Ave Maria" without a care in the world, his place firmly marked by a semi-sticky little note. Perhaps a little slow on the uptake, 3M didn't introduce the Post-It Notes until 1977, and when they did, people just didn't get the idea and the product floundered. But persistence paid off. One year later, 3M inundated the Boise, Idaho, market with Post-It Note samples. After trying the notes, nine out of ten people said they'd purchase the product . . . if only they had a little note affixed somewhere to remind them. A decade or so after their introduction, Post-It Notes were stuck everywhere.

The little notes quickly changed people's organizational behavior. In the 1990s, Post-It Notes sales reached $15 billion. To date, 3M has sold an excess of 1 trillion sticky notes. Widely considered one of the most important inventions of the twentieth century, they have even been displayed in the Museum of Modern Art.

Fry has since received many accolades for his role in revolutionizing office communication. Today, Fry travels the world to speak on the topics of creativity and innovation. And you? Well, I'll bet your friends got a big kick out of the clever name you came up with for your pet rock. "Rocky Horror" was it? Yeah. *Very* clever.

2   BARBED WIRE

TAGLINE: A *really* pointy fence

PREDECESSOR: Fences that didn't hurt

LESSON: Better fences make better neighbors.

Have you ever urinated outdoors? No? For the sake of brevity, let's dispense with the formality of pretending you're not lying. As someone who's peed outdoors, you've probably been in a scenario where you just "gotta go," so you creep into the woods only to be stopped by thorny bushes and are forced to go elsewhere. Essentially, that is how barbed wire works, only without the pee.

People are often surprised when told that barbed wire is considered one of the most significant inventions of the past 200 years. But barbed wire is held in this high regard for one reason: the cow.

See, back in the days of the Wild West, livestock grazed freely. Before the introduction of the "thorny fence" (as barbed wire is also known), wild and domesticated animals simply penetrated existing fence systems and had their way with crops. Think about it. If one little bunny can gnaw his way through your carefully cultivated lettuce patch, imagine the damage that could be done by 10,000 head of 1,500-pound cattle!

It was Lucien B. Smith who helped rein in the livestock. He received the first patent for barbed wire in 1867. Joseph F. Glidden improved on the concept and was issued a patent for his modified version in 1874.

The widespread use of this highly effective fencing method changed life in the west almost as dramatically as line dancing and the gigantic belt buckle. Without this extraordinarily simple invention, U.S. agriculture would have been severely stunted, making western migration and the settlement of the majority of the United States impossible.

3 | GOLF

PREDECESSOR: Strolling about un-aggravated

LESSON: Necessity's not always the mother of invention . . . in this case, it's not even a third cousin.

Have you ever whacked a rock with a stick? Well, then congratulations, you could have invented golf.

In fact, this pastime is so simple that it was invented a full three *centuries* before mankind entertained the idea that the earth revolved around the sun. And, like so many other inventions, it appears to be the direct result of boredom.

Details are a little sketchy, but as far as historians can tell, around the mid-1300s, the advent of golf went something like this . . .

> **Bored Scotsman #1:** Hey, Angus, I'll bet you a sheep's bladder I can get this rock into that wee lil' hole over there using only my staff, in fewer tries than it takes you to do the same.
> **Bored Scotsman #2:** Why the hell would I want to do that?
> **Bored Scotsman #1:** Beats working.

They then proceeded to do just that until dusk.

And that, more or less, is how you begin and end a game of golf today, give or take a sheep entrail.

By 1447, the game became so popular that Scottish men were neglecting archery practice—not a good idea when those pesky British were sniffing around the kingdom's borders again. For this reason, King James II banned the game for fear of invasion. (This is the first recorded contact that golf had with Nike . . . though not the shoe company, the actual Goddess of Victory.) Seriously though, within 100 years golf was so popular it got the entire Kingdom of Scotland in trouble with their boss, and it's been doing it with golfers ever since.

That's One Small Step for Man . . .

They've been called "the ugliest shoes ever made," "tinker toys on steroids," and "rubber abominations," but do the inventors mind this criticism? Who knows? They can't stop laughing long enough for anyone to ask them.

Today, Crocs Shoes are available all over the world and are one of the most successful shoe stories in the history of footwear. That's one small step for man, one giant, ugly, leap for mankind.

4 CROCS

TAGLINE: Cheap, hideous, rubber footwear

PREDECESSOR: Ugly shoes that people didn't want to buy

LESSON: It doesn't have to be pretty; it just has to be good.

It is said, "There are no stupid questions." Sure, it's usually said by someone who wants to make stupid people feel better, but there is truth in that statement. And if you need proof, look no farther then the shoe sensation: Crocs.

On a Caribbean sailing trip in May 2002, three, allegedly, inebriated Colorado guys asked themselves, "If we could conceive of the perfect shoe, what would it be?" Their answer: A shoe they could wear on their boating trips that was comfortable, practical, and fun. Taking it a few ugly steps further, they opined that this "wonder shoe" should be slip-proof, waterproof, and not leave scuffmarks, and shouldn't smell after getting wet.

When they sobered up it still seemed like a pretty good idea. So, with strictly utilitarian needs in mind, they designed a simple rubber shoe. The shoe was made of nonscuffing durable rubber. Nothing new, really. But then to achieve comfort and aeration they made the shoe wide and roomy and added ventilation holes (which leads one to question their definition of "waterproof shoe"). They ended up with an extremely good shoe for its designated purpose, and in July 2002 they debuted them at a local boat show.

What happened next is the stuff of invention legend. People took to the strange footwear as one might take to a puppy that's so ugly it's cute. Their homeliness became an instant asset. That coupled with their undeniable comfort and usefulness drove demand through the roof, and by 2003 they could barely keep up with the deluge of orders.

Approximately 45,000,000 yo-yos were sold in 1962.

5 | YO-YO

TAGLINE: A toy you toss and it returns

PREDECESSOR: A toy you toss and it breaks

LESSON: Deadly weapons *do* make great kids' toys.

Allow me to apologize in advance for the following: The yo-yo has had its ups and downs.

Once again we find ourselves examining ingenuity through the recognition of a good idea, rather than the actual invention of an object. A lot of people assume that D. F. Duncan invented the yo-yo. But he most certainly did not. In fact, the yo-yo had been around for over two *centuries* before Duncan made it popular.

It first made its way to the Western world in the 1800s, where the fancy-schmancy British referred to it as the *quiz* and *bandalore*, which was adopted from the French who also called the ancient toy an *incroyable*. Clearly not as catchy as *yo-yo*. However, Duncan didn't even come up with that name. It's actually the term used in the toy's native Philippines, and translates to "Come back!"

Even better, the toy was actually used as a weapon on the island nation for over 400 years. A little different than the one you use to walk the dog, their version came complete with sharp edges and points—perfect for flinging at enemies and prey. Granted, it didn't stand a chance against the colonizer's weapons, which is probably why it's no coincidence they were a conquered people for about 400 years.

But back to the yo-yo you know today . . . it took D. F. Duncan Sr.'s recognition of the toy's potential in order for it to become a must-have for every American kid. The company's advertising campaigns caused millions to flock to stores in search of the deadly weapon-turned-child's toy. The yo-yo's popularity peaked in 1962 when forty-five million of them were sold, though it remains a favorite for the four-foot set. Unfortunately, mismanagement bankrupted Duncan's company around this same time. So Duncan cut the string (and his losses). The Flambeau Plastic Company dropped in and bought Duncan's shares as well as the rights to his name and his trademarks in 1968.

So Is It *Duck* Tape or *Duct* Tape?

It's both.

Because of its waterproof qualities, military personnel referred to the tape as "duck tape." After the war, construction workers used it on air-conditioning and heating ducts. Hence the slight change in the name from *duck* to *duct*.

6   DUCT TAPE

TAGLINE: Super sticky silver tape

PREDECESSOR: Repairing things properly

LESSON: If your product can hold the universe together, you're on the right track.

Jury rigging, or *Jerry rigging* as it's sometimes known, has been in existence since prehistoric man hastily repaired his woolly mammoth-trunk shower-head with the very first roll of duct tape . . . oh wait . . . that was a *Flintstones* episode. Nevertheless, man has made an art form out of the quick fix, and the invention of duct tape brought him a brand new way of hastily slapping things together.

The story of duct tape starts with the invention of adhesive—the *sticky* in the *super sticky silver tape.* This sticky substance is a complicated chemical concoction, and therefore not included as an item in this book. However, its application in the form of duct tape is simplistic brilliance.

The first people to turn the adhesive into the duct tape we know and love today were the sticky-fingered hotshots in the Johnson and Johnson Permacel Division in 1942. While duct tape's original use was to keep moisture out of ammunition cases during World War II, military personnel found it to be a quick fix for just about any problem. Soldiers used it on everything from their artillery to their vehicles

After the war ended, the decision was made to change the tape's color from Army green to civilian silver since it was intended for use on metal ducts. Although, just as soldiers did during the war, people found that its strength, versatility, and durability made it useful for all sorts of things throughout the home.

Today, duct tape is one of the most widely sold adhesive products in the world and remains an essential part of any home tool kit.

DID YOU KNOW ?

While the guillotine is probably best known for its use during France's Reign of Terror (when it was used on King Louis XVI and Marie Antoinette), the machine was also employed during World War II. According to the A&E television program *Modern Marvels: Death Devices*, the Nazis used the guillotine on 16,500 people in Germany and Austria between 1933 and 1945.

7 GUILLOTINE

TAGLINE: Head severing device

PREDECESSOR: Hanging, stoning, bludgeoning, drowning, pummeling, hacking . . .

LESSON: If you want 'em dead, find a tidy way to behead.

Gruesome? Sure. But the cold hard fact is: Humans have been trying to find simple, efficient ways to execute one another since before recorded time. And a lot of recorded times it didn't go so well.

Hanging was the most popular form of execution and definitely no picnic. To note just one of many examples, witnesses received quite a surprise at the 1906 execution of William Williamson. When the trap door swung open, William fell all the way to the ground and landed on his feet. (Seems his executioner was a little tipsy.) Can you imagine that? You're waiting to have your neck snapped and you land on your feet. *Whew!* That's a Get Out of Jail Free card, right? Wrong. Three deputies, standing on the scaffold, seized the rope and forcibly pulled William off the floor for fourteen and a half minutes until the coroner pronounced him dead from strangulation. Now, *that* is a bad day.

Axe for a Better Way to Go?
In 1541, it took three strokes of an axe to sever the head of Margaret, Countess of Salisbury. Trees have been brought down quicker than that.

Countless instances of human error in legally snuffing people out, led Tobias Schmidt, a German engineer, to let gravity and a blade do the work when he invented the guillotine in the eighteenth century.

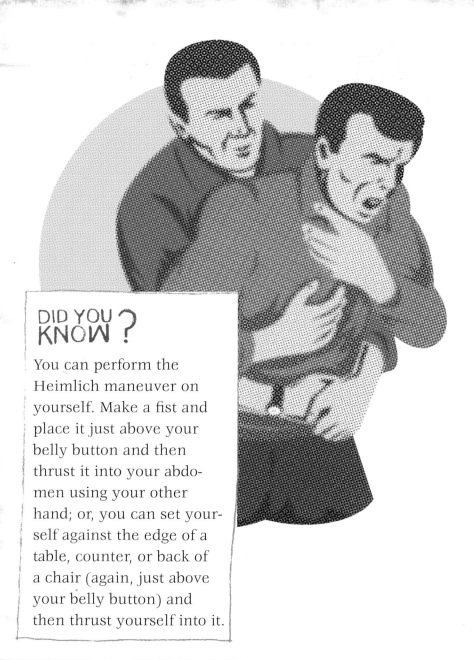

DID YOU KNOW ?

You can perform the Heimlich maneuver on yourself. Make a fist and place it just above your belly button and then thrust it into your abdomen using your other hand; or, you can set yourself against the edge of a table, counter, or back of a chair (again, just above your belly button) and then thrust yourself into it.

8 THE HEIMLICH MANEUVER

TAGLINE: Squeezing bits of food out of embarrassed diners

PREDECESSOR: Inadvertently jamming the foreign object further down people's throats by pounding on their backs

LESSON: Eating and breathing don't jibe very well.

Ronald Reagan
Cher
Dick Vitale
Halle Berry

What do these people have in common? They've all allegedly been saved from choking by one Henry Heimlich, MD, who introduced the procedure in 1974.

While the footage would make fascinating YouTube fodder, these famous folks aren't the only people who've inadvertently sucked down hunks of food into their larynxes. Plenty of average people have managed to send their suppers down the wrong pipe, only to be saved by the Heimlich maneuver. It's estimated that the Heimlich has saved more than 50,000 people. Why? Because people talk with their mouths full, that's why! Listen to your mothers!

So you know that the Heimlich works, but what about *how* it works? Well it's as simple as a spitball. Have you ever launched a spitball across a room? Stop it. Of course you have. The spitball goes into the straw at one end then it's shot across the room by blowing through the other. Like the spitball prin-

THE HEIMLICH HAS SAVED MORE THAN 50,000 PEOPLE.

ciple, the food goes down the choker's windpipe and then is shot out when the squeezer grabs the choker from behind and applies pressure to the diaphragm with an abominable thrust. Simple as that.

By 1928,
Epperson earned royalties on more
than 60,000,000 ice pops.

9   POPSICLE

TAGLINE: A sweet frozen treat

PREDECESSOR: Juice

LESSON: Freeze treats.

How many times have you placed a warm drink in the freezer to cool it down only to forget about it and find it frozen solid hours later? An innocent and annoying mistake to you, a gold mine to one eleven-year-old Frank Epperson. In 1905, he left his beverage outside overnight on the porch of his Oakland, California, home. It froze and the stick he had used to stir it stuck in place. So did the idea. He named it the Epperson icicle, which of course didn't stick.

> "It's not what you look at that matters, it's what you see."
>
> **—HENRY DAVID THOREAU**

The following summer, he recreated the treats in his family's fridge and sold them around town, under the shortened name: Epsicle. Epperson finally patented his treat in 1924 under the name Popsicle, which came from his children's frequent requests for their Pop's sickles.

By 1928, Epperson had sold the rights to the name Popsicle and earned royalties on more than sixty million ice pops. That's a pretty cool profit for accidentally leaving a drink on your back porch. Makes you wonder how much money some of your stupid mistakes could make you, doesn't it?

Today, popsicles are made and distributed by a number of different companies in a number of different shapes and flavors. However, the trademark Popsicle belongs to the Unilever corporation that distributes the flavored ice under the Popsicle brand name.

OVER 1,200 PATENTS HAVE
BEEN ISSUED FOR
BREAST-SUPPORTING
DEVICES.

10 BRA

Abbott and Costello, airbags, babaloos, bazoomas, Ben and Jerry, Bert and Ernie, blinkers, cans, cha-chas, chesticles, chumbawumbas, coconuts, gazongas, Holmes and Watson, honkers, hooters, jahoobies, jugs, knockers, melons, a pair, palookas, rack, shabba-dos, tatas, torpedoes, Tweedledee and Tweedledum, wahwahs, whimwhams, Winnebagos, wopbopaloobops, yahoos . . . call 'em what you want to call 'em, any way you swing 'em, they've been supported by bras since 2500 B.C.

For centuries women have had a desire to enhance the shape of their bosom for mostly aesthetic reasons. Actually, I should probably put it this way: For centuries men have wanted to look at cleavage and women have obliged.

The breast supporting philosophy changed slightly during the nineteenth century when women sought more comfortable underwear than the trussed and squeezed look of that day's corset. You might say it was an upheaval. As new undergarment creations came on the market, patents were issued at a rapid rate. The U.S. government has granted 1,200 patents for bra-like inventions since the first "corset substitute" was issued in 1863. Being a "supporter of breasts" myself, I think that's great.

In 1893 Marie Tucek received a patent for what was literally called the "breast supporter." It had two separate cups with straps over the shoulders and was fastened by a hook-and-eye closure in the back. Tucek's patent remains the basis of the modern bra, yet unhooking it still baffles men to this day.

THE MODERN CAN OPENER
WAS PATENTED SIXTY
YEARS AFTER CANNED
FOOD. GOOD THING IT
KEEPS, HUH?

11 | CAN OPENER

TAGLINE: A quick fix when you want to fix dinner quick

PREDECESSOR: Chisel and hammer

LESSON: Think ahead.

The invention of the can opener is a story of thick metal and even thicker heads. You would think the creation of the can opener would time closely to the creation of canned food. You would think that . . . but you'd be wrong.

Peter Durand patented the concept of canning food in 1810. And he used the British Navy to help test the longevity of the canned food's edibility. Durand was all, "Check it out—food stays fresh" and the Navy was all "Cheerio then!" But it wasn't until they were in the middle of the ocean that they were like, "Blimey! How in the bloody hell do we open these things?"*

See, Durand figured out how to seal stuff in really well, but he didn't really think through how to remove it. His cans' instructions read: Cut round the top near the outer edge with a chisel and hammer. (I wonder if he even bothered to label the contents?)

It took an American inventor to figure it out. (Score one for us Yanks.) Ezra Warner received a patent for his can opener in 1858. The invention resembled a bent bayonet, and was used by first puncturing the can with its point and then dragging it around the rim. A little more work than the one you have in your kitchen today.

Our modern can opener (the one with the crank and wheel that does most of the work for us) wasn't invented until 1870. It too was invented by an American, William Lyman. He made it possible for the novice to use the device, which led to mass consumption that, of course, led to one rich Mr. Lyman.

So, the modern can opener was patented 60 years after canned food. Good thing it keeps, huh?

* I've taken *just a little* artistic license in recounting how the Durand/Navy/can-opener relationship went down.

WHAM-O SOLD 25,000,000
HULA HOOPS IN THE FIRST FOUR MONTHS.

12 | HULA HOOP

TAGLINE: An excuse to gyrate . . . well . . . another excuse to gyrate

PREDECESSOR: Hula-ing . . . without the hoop

LESSON: You don't have to invent it to make millions from it.

Think the Hula Hoop was a '50s thing? Guess again. Only the marketing ploy came from that decade. In fact, people have been gyrating with circular hoops for some time now. The idea can be traced all the way back to ancient Egypt where children played with large rings of dried grapevines. (I swear. Check out Stephen Goode's article, "Did Egyptians Know How to Do the Hula?") And the first Hoop trend didn't hit during the doo-wop era; it actually happened in fourteenth-century England. Doctors' records from that period credit the craze as the cause of back pains and heart attacks.

Even the term "hula hoop" wasn't a '50s original. That happened in the 1800s when British sailors were the first to attach "hula" to "hoop." After visiting Hawaii, they noted the similarity between the natives' hula dancing and their own gyrations. The natives subsequently slaughtered the sailors, but that's a whole other story . . .

The real innovation in this case isn't the actual invention, but the *recognition* that the concept had sales potential. And this recognition came from where else but Wham-O—a California toy manufacturer that appears repeatedly throughout this book. Wham-O marketed the hell out of the Hoop; their marketers literally hit the pavement as they began holding Hula Hoop demonstrations at playgrounds throughout the country. Shortly after Wham-O's campaign began in 1958, the concept caught on and spread—fast. Twenty-five million Hula Hoops flew off store shelves in the first four months alone.

Like any fad, though, the Hula Hoop craze cooled. By the early '60s kids were clamoring for the next big thing. However, that doesn't mean the Hoop didn't stick around. Even today, they're still being used in backyards and playgrounds. Think about it: Who *hasn't* Hula Hooped? So here's to a creation that's a big fat invitation for worldwide gyration.

13 THE NECKTIE

TAGLINE: Useless ribbons of fabric awkwardly fastened to men's necks

PREDECESSOR: Freedom

LESSON: Where fashion is concerned, useless is priceless.

Men are known even less for accessorizing than they are for their attention to detail. Incredibly this has not stopped us from fastening colored and often fancily patterned ribbons around our necks for the past 2,000 years.

Throughout human history, men and women have adorned their bodies with neckwear. It all began *way* back when ancient Egyptian men would hang a rectangular piece of cloth around their shoulders as a symbol of social status.

The use of the necktie evolved over the years and was often used as part of military uniforms. (Presumably to over accessorize the enemy into submission.) In the late eighteenth century, a looser version of the necktie known as a *cravat* was introduced into mainstream fashion by a group of young men called the Macaronis. These were young Englishmen who, upon returning from countries such as Italy—that's where the "macaroni" part comes in—brought back new ideas for menswear and fashion.

So we have those English lads to thank for coming to town a-riding on some ponies. Then, presumably, not satisfied with merely sticking feathers in their caps, tying scarves around their necks and calling themselves Macaronis.

But if there is a single figure who most profited from the advancement of the necktie and is responsible for its modern look and use, we must fast forward to the 1920s when manufacturer Jesse Langsdorf created a "wrinkle free" tie which could be easily worn to the office by the increasing number of professional men. Thanks Jesse!

Today millions of these strips of cloth are sold each year in the United States alone. Let's not even get started on the clip-on . . .

When the Scott Paper Company first manufactured toilet paper, it declined to put its company name anywhere on the product's packaging.

14 | PAPER TOWEL

TAGLINE: Disposable absorbent cloth

PREDECESSOR: Nondisposable absorbent cloth

LESSON: Convenience is king.

The paper towel! Perhaps the most wasteful household item in the history of mankind. Before this whole "save the earth" business got started, I would rip off a paper towel and throw it in the trash each time I walked by the roll for no reason whatsoever other than force of habit. Nevertheless it has made quite an impact over the years.

The history of paper towels all starts with a railroad car full of toilet paper. You see, a trainload of toilet tissue was on its way out from the Scott Paper Company in 1907 when the company president received some unpleasant news. The paper in the railcar was *too thick* to be used as toilet paper. (I can't make this stuff up . . . well, most of it, anyway.) Now, not to provide too much personal information, but I can use just about any thickness when the need arises. So I don't know what kind of alarmist gave the chief that call. But anyway, the president had a plan.

Determined to prevent this thickness issue from hurting his bottom line, he instructed his people to cut the too-thick tissue into larger sections for non–ass related wiping. And thus the Scott Sani-Towel was born, marketed as a more hygienic alternative to the germ-filled cloth rags people were using to clean their kitchens. You'd think they'd fly off the shelves, but it seems people back then weren't too concerned about spreading salmonella all over their countertops. It wasn't until 1931 when the perforated version we know and love today was introduced that people started paying attention to the product.

15 CABBAGE PATCH KIDS

TAGLINE: Creepy dolls with birth certificates

PREDECESSOR: Undocumented, less creepy dolls

LESSON: Apparently in the 1980s, kids really liked creepy dolls.

It's Christmastime 1983. Styx is confusing the nation by thanking "Mr. Roboto" in Japanese. Robert Wagner and his TV wife are stumbling upon at least one murder each week in *Hart to Hart*, and Ronald Reagan's hair is *perfect*.

Meanwhile in toy stores across the nation, grown men and women are scratching, biting, kicking, and cursing at one another in fierce competition over the Cabbage Patch Kids. Everyone *had* to have one under the Christmas tree for their kids. After all it was the 80s. Everybody *had* to have *everything*!

The hoopla all started back in 1976 when Xavier Roberts invented the Little Person dolls. They were the older brothers and sisters to the Cabbage Patch Kids. Just a teenager at the time, Roberts ran the Babyland General Hospital out of his home in Cleveland, Georgia. (Safe to assume Roberts didn't play a whole lot of sports, don't you think?) This was the place, creepily enough, where doll-lovers could "adopt" his Little Person offspring. Never referred to as dolls, Roberts's "babies" were hand sewn and came with adoption papers. A little strange when you see it in writing . . . but the Coleco toy company saw something in Roberts's invention. They bought the rights to the doll . . . *sorry* . . . Little Person line and started marketing them as Cabbage Patch Kids in 1983. And that's when all hell broke loose.

After a huge initial success (which included parents rioting in local toy stores), Coleco went bankrupt in 1988. Babyland General Hospital relocated to Hasbro and then again to Mattel in 1994. The rights to the baby-making factory were sold again in 2003 when Toys "R" Us took control of the brand. All these creepy little things wanted were homes, yet they were relocated more than real kids in today's social services system.

MORE THAN
100,000,000,000
BAND-AIDs
HAVE BEEN SOLD.

16 BAND-AID

TAGLINE: A little piece of tape with some gauze stuck to it

PREDECESSOR: Tiny wound overkill

LESSON: Stop blood loss.

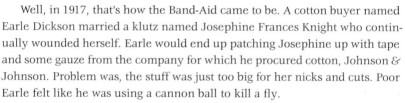

We all know somebody who's clumsy—banging into stuff, falling down a lot—the kind of person who scares the hell out of you when he handles a knife or, *God forbid*, does that leaning-back-in-a-chair thing.

And, we all know a Boy Scout or two.

Well, in 1917, that's how the Band-Aid came to be. A cotton buyer named Earle Dickson married a klutz named Josephine Frances Knight who continually wounded herself. Earle would end up patching Josephine up with tape and some gauze from the company for which he procured cotton, Johnson & Johnson. Problem was, the stuff was just too big for her nicks and cuts. Poor Earle felt like he was using a cannon ball to kill a fly.

So Earle made a batch of little bandages by affixing pre-cut squares of Johnson & Johnson sterile gauze to some little bits of surgical tape. He found some fabric called Conaline, which he used to cover the sticky parts of the tape so the bandages wouldn't start sticking before they were supposed to. The little devils worked so well that he presented the idea to his boss, James Johnson, who ordered production to begin in 1920.

At first, sales were slow. Then, somebody had the idea to distribute free samples to Boy Scout troops, which, as you know, are just teeming with adolescent boys running around in sharp, pointy forests wearing short pants. Brilliant!

The little invention took off and, to date, more than one hundred billion Band-Aids have been sold. Well done Earle, well done.

A Toilet by Any Other Name Still Smells

If the word *toilet* just isn't titillating enough for you, there is no shortage of other names for it . . . privy, loo, washroom, commode, lavatory, shitter, porcelain throne, potty, dump, black hole, rest room, powder room, john, lav, little boys' room, little girls' room, water closet, bog, the oval office, the thinking chair, the reading room, turd pool, porcelain king, Super Bowl, turd tube, and the boom-boom room.

17 | TOILET BOWL

TAGLINE: Bowl in which one defecates

PREDECESSOR: Everywhere else

LESSON: Ya gotta do what ya gotta do, so make it easier for people to do it.

Latrine, restroom, can, crapper, John, and so on and so on—the number of names for this extremely simple device suggests only one thing: No one actually wants to say what it's for. And for the purposes of this book I'm not going to say it's a receptacle for the efficient disposal of adult human feces either.

Like any good invention, there's some disagreement over who should be credited with the invention of the modern toilet. Though the controversy continues to swirl about (clockwise here in the States . . . counterclockwise in Australia), I've flushed out two main contenders. Most experts agree that J. F. Brondel introduced the first valve-type flush toilet in 1738. However John Harrington is credited with inventing the "water closet" 150 years earlier. But Harrington's version was not as closely related to our modern toilet, though it did have a flushing mechanism.

So despite what many people think, Sir Thomas Crapper did *not* invent the toilet. However, Thomas Crapper was issued nine patents; four were for drain improvements, three for "water closets," one for manhole covers, and one for pipe joints. So, if you think about it, it's not a huge leap to associate Tommy with the word "crap."

To plop an American Tommy into the invention mix, Thomas Jefferson invented an indoor toilet at his residence, Monticello, by rigging a system of pulleys. Servants (also known as his "slaves" or his "children") used the device to haul away chamber pots.

> **Toilets in Outer Space!**
> In 1981 NASA developed an advanced waste management system for the space shuttle that utilizes suction to . . . well you get the idea.

DID YOU KNOW?

Early Romans used porcu-pine quills as toothpicks.

18 TOOTHPICK

TAGLINE: A little pointy stick

PREDECESSOR: Loud sucking noises

LESSON: Make it easier for people to do something they already do.

Food has been getting stuck in people's teeth for over 400,000 years. Neanderthal and *Homo sapiens* fossils show clear signs that even early humans picked their teeth with rudimentary tools. So you'd think some caveman would have opened up a little toothpick emporium way back in the d-a-y. Lord knows if the *Flintstones* taught us anything, it's that prehistoric man was a sucker for get-rich-quick schemes. But it wasn't until 1858 that somebody figured out how to take toothpicks all the way to the bank.

Charles Forster of Strong, Maine, is believed to be the first person to manufacture toothpicks. And it wasn't as easy as you'd think. He had to go all the way to South America to figure it out. In his travels, Forster watched natives use little pieces of wood to clean their teeth. Impressed by the technology that had been under our collective noses for 400 millennia, he sent a sample box home to his wife who showed them around. "Check these out!" she said to the people of Maine, who stared back at her dumbly and made sucking noises in an effort to dislodge the food from their teeth. After a quick and disgusting, demonstration, Mr. Foster had more orders than you could shake a tiny little stick at—especially from hotels and restaurants.

Foster's first few batches were handmade; the Model T of toothpicks you might say. But by 1860, he had to devise machines to keep up with the growing demand. The genius of the toothpick-making machine was that it allowed sticks to be cut into, uh, much smaller sticks.

Today, there are toothpicks-a-plenty in nearly every household and eating establishment in the world. Their dental applications aside, without them our club sandwiches would be completely unmanageable, our fingers would be all over those free samples at Costco, and our tropical drinks would be lackluster in the absence of tiny paper umbrellas.

Over 100,000,000,000,000
PAPER CLIPS HAVE BEEN SOLD.

19 PAPER CLIP

TAGLINE: The staple for people with commitment issues

PREDECESSOR: A straight pin stuck into stacks of paper

LESSON: Most people are unorganized. Organize them.

We have all reverse engineered a paper clip at one point in our lives, only to discover that our suspicions were correct: It's a wire.

Wire was invented as early as 1500 B.C., so why did it take so long to make this mental leap? Lots of reasons . . . steel wire was still new, machinery had to be introduced to manufacture it, and so on. But mainly, it's because you, or someone like you, didn't think of it until the 1860s when Samuel B. Fay made millions from the idea. It's this type of tiny, cricket-sized mental leap that separates the everyday entrepreneur from the billionaire. All you have to do is get out your tiny mental cricket and give him a little shove.

> "Many of life's failures are people who did not realize how close they were to success when they gave up."
>
> —THOMAS EDISON

Fay patented the paper clip in 1867. The original patent listed its primary purpose as attaching tickets to fabric, but it did make mention that it could be used to organize papers. A subsequent flood of paper clip patents was issued beginning in 1868 as hundreds of would-be inventors were audibly heard striking their foreheads and saying, "D-oh!"

Nowadays you can't sit at your desk without seeing at least one paper clip, which to date have sold over 100 trillion units. It's amazing to think that people have purchased that many pieces of bent wire. But it goes to show that a great idea will go a great distance.

20 WHEEL

TAGLINE: A round cylinder

PREDECESSOR: Dragging stuff

LESSON: You may be looking at the greatest invention ever without realizing it.

I get it—the wheel is probably the most important mechanical invention of all time. But *come on!* How hard was it to figure out? I mean even during the Stone Ages stuff rolled, didn't it? Some caveman must've noticed a log or a rock rolling down a hill. Hell, it probably happened all the time! However, it took quite some time to work out the principle that round things roll. And for many cultures it eluded them entirely until nearly *modern times*!

Because the concept behind the wheel appears to be so simple, one might assume that people would naturally pick up on it. But incredibly, this is not the case. The Inca, Aztec, and Maya cultures were highly advanced, yet they never used the wheel. In fact, there is no evidence that the wheel existed in Western civilizations until after the Europeans came over to decimate them.

The very first wheel was most likely made of a section of wooden log. Later, more advanced tools made it possible to carve wheels from stone. The first flat tire followed shortly thereafter.

Today the wheel is so commonplace it is barely noticed. However, aside from the obvious applications for transport vehicles such as cars, trucks and trains, etc., we are dependent upon the wheel in many less obvious ways. In fact, nearly every piece of machinery created uses a form of wheel in its mechanisms. From watches to turbine engines, modern society would grind to a halt like a rusty gear without this simplest of contraptions.

"Perhaps imagination is only
intelligence having fun."

—**GEORGE SCIALABBA**

21 | BIKINI

TAGLINE: Wearing your underwear in public

PREDECESSOR: Wearing your underwear in private

LESSON: Being first isn't everything. And sex sells.

Talk about a no-brainer. If you were to take every heterosexual male who has ever been born and raise them, individually, in complete isolation, each and every one of them would independently invent the bikini . . . about three seconds before they invented the naked lady. But it wasn't until 1946 that someone cashed in on the male lust for barely there, soaking-wet attire, and did so with a little help from the Atomic Bomb.

Don't get me wrong; running around naked at the beach is nothing new. Women have done it for ages. But sadly by 1946, the liberal attitude toward the scantily clad female form had disappeared and bathing suits looked more like nuns' habits. That's where two Frenchmen come in.

Jacques Heim first advertised his two-piece bathing suit over the skies of Cannes, calling it the *atome* (French for atom) because of how small it was. Three weeks later, Louis Reard unveiled his two-piece number. Using skywriters over the beaches of the Riviera, he proclaimed his suit, "Smaller than the smallest bathing suit in the world," and named it the bikini. Reard spun a story about how the name bikini came from the little islands in the South Pacific where the United States recently tested several nuclear weapons. The bikini, he said, was named so because he had "split the atom." Very clever.

Don't laugh. Take a product that allows women to run around nearly naked, throw them into a post world war society teaming with sexual tension, add a storyline that links the whole thing to the nuclear bomb, stir in a pun or two or five thousand, and *voila*! You have headlines all over the world and a place in history.

As Heim found out, you can come up with an idea first, and still get scooped. Besides, "Itsy Bitsy Teeny Weeny Yellow Polka-Dot *Atome*?" That's clunky. Okay, now you can laugh.

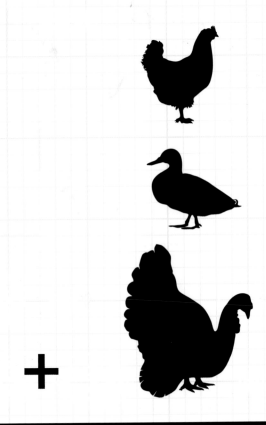

+

_____

= **turducken**

THE TURDUCKEN DOES NOT OCCUR
NATURALLY IN THE WILD.

22 | TURDUCKEN

TAGLINE: An ungodly combination of birds

PREDECESSOR: Eating poultry one species at a time

LESSON: No idea is too weird.

A guy walks into a butcher shop with a turkey, a chicken, and a duck . . . . No, this is not a joke—it's the *turducken*.

Not since the "refried bean" has boredom been the catalyst for such culinary delight. Three boned, stuffed birds, crammed into one another: a turkey stuffed with a duck, stuffed with a chicken. The turducken is food gone a-fowl.

A meal consisting of three life forms, fused, as if by some hideous matter transfer experiment, may seem more like a zoological discovery than an invention, but I assure you, the turducken does not occur naturally in the wild.

Apparently, one day in 1985, a man whose name has been lost to history, strolled into Hebert's Specialty Meats in Maurice, Louisiana, carrying three birds and instructed the staff there to build him one turducken. Mercifully, the procedure was performed post-mortem. Once word got out that there was a way to kill, mangle, and then eat three animals at once, the demand went through the roof.

Since its creation, the turducken has rapidly grown in popularity. The company now sells around 16,000 turduckens a year. They share a friendly rivalry with Paul Prudhomme's 75,000 turduckens-per-year, retailing anywhere from $75 to $250. And those are only the professionally prepared turduckens—it doesn't include the thousands of turduckens prepared each year by amateurs.

If ever you blew a chance to invent something when you were high, this was it. But, hey, it's not too late. Surely you can cram a Cornish game hen into that chicken and then maybe a parakeet into that?

Good luck.

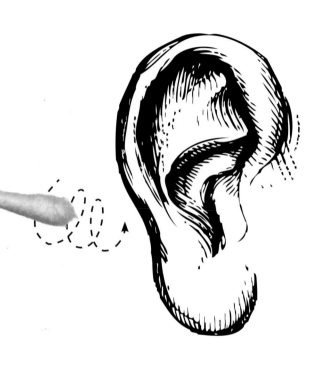

APPROXIMATELY 26,000,000,000 Q-TIPS ARE SOLD EVERY YEAR.

23 Q-TIPS

TAGLINE: A stick with some cotton on it*

PREDECESSOR: Dirty ears

LESSON: Indispensable, disposable products mean repeat customers.

Perhaps one of the most blatant examples of corporate denial is this statement on every box of Q-Tips: Do not insert in ear canal.

Please.

Despite this warning, people have been sticking these things in their ear canals since 1920, when a Polish-born American named Leo Gerstenzang invented them to prevent his wife from sticking toothpicks (p. 35) in their newborn infant's ear canal.

Allow me to explain.

Leo's wife had rigged up a different device to clean their baby's ears at bath time—a toothpick stuck into a piece of cotton. Leo decided that it probably wasn't a good idea to insert something into his child's ear that had the word "pick" in its name, so he designed a ready-made cotton swab that would do the same with a lot less risk. And thus the Q-Tip was born. Well, not exactly. He named his product: The Gerstenzang Infant Novelty Company's Baby Gays.

Now, I know what you're thinking. You're thinking, "not only could I have invented that but I certainly would have named it differently. I mean, 'Infant Novelty'? What's *that* all about?"

Well, Leo felt the same way, eventually changing the name to Q-Tips Baby Gays, with the Q standing for "Quality" and the "Gay" standing for "Homosexual." *Kidding, kidding . . .* though when the Schwab Company purchased the brand, Baby Gays was dropped along with the product's exclusive use for infant care. Q-Tips are now one of the biggest selling personal care products on the planet. Schwab sells twenty-six billion Q-Tips per year and remains in denial about the "ear canal" thing.

 * Which under no circumstances (*nudge, nudge*) should you insert in your ear canal (*wink, wink*).

Belgian Embassy: Hello, Belgian Embassy, this is Océane. How can we help you? (She then repeated the former greeting in Dutch.)

Me: Quick question Océane, who invented the sliced potato boiled in oil?

Océane (in a cute accent): Ah, excellent question. Belgium has historical evidence that we were eating potato strips fried in oil as early as the seventeenth century.

Me: You mean, French fries?

Océane: Ja.

Me: *Ah ha!*

24 | FRENCH FRIES

TAGLINE: Potato slices thrown into boiling oil

PREDECESSOR: Whole potatoes thrown into boiling water

LESSON: If you deep-fry it, they will come.

The French insist that they invented the French fry—the Belgians say it was them. So in the interest of fairness, I called the Belgian Embassy and inquired about its creation (see page 46).

Based on my extensive research, which consisted of tricking a Belgian receptionist into recognizing fried potato strips as French fries, I'm going to go with the French side of the story. Plus, the Belgians already have that delicious waffle named after them.

And on top of my conversation with Océane, our very own Thomas Jefferson backed up the French claim. Now Jefferson wasn't "Washington honest"—as evidenced by all those slave children who looked like him—but there isn't any evidence that he lied about fried foods. A menu was found from one of Jefferson's dinner parties held in 1801, which clearly states that his guests would be served "potatoes, deep fried, and served in the French way." This was risky because potatoes back then were thought to be highly poisonous unless boiled thoroughly. Jefferson assured his guests that his French Chef, Honoré Julien, would prepare the potatoes in a manner that would not kill them, and they did not.

Yes, it seems it was a Frenchman who came up with the extraordinarily simple revelation that potatoes taste good after being fried in a vat of oil.

But then, doesn't everything?

"Don't worry about people stealing your ideas. If your ideas are any good, you'll have to ram them down people's throats."

—**HOWARD H. AIKEN**

25 | WIRE HANGER

TAGLINE: Mangled and twisted piece of wire

PREDECESSOR: Wooden hangers

LESSON: Be careful. Protect yourself and your idea.

In a pinch, they help us break into automobiles, unclog our toilets, and faithfully serve as old car radio and television antennas. But, mainly, they provide an inexpensive hanging place for nearly any article of clothing, except fancy, little-girl dresses (according to Joan Crawford). And it's all thanks to Albert J. Parkhouse.

Like every other morning, Albert arrived to work one day in 1903 at the Timberlake Wire and Novelty Company, a Michigan company that made lampshade frames and other wire items. Flush with excitement at the prospect of making lampshade skeletons and other wire novelties for painfully low wages, he went to hang his hat and coat on the hooks considerately provided by the company. But all the hooks were in use.

He thought about just wearing his coat, but the prospect of getting a sleeve caught in the machinery convinced him otherwise. After all, maimed workers were sent home early, without pay. Ever the dedicated worker-bee, Parkhouse picked up a piece of wire, bent it into two large hoops and twisted both ends at the center to create a hook. He hung up his coat and began his workday.

What did Albert get for his vigilance?

His boss, John B. Timberlake, happened by, no doubt on his way to count his money, and promptly took out a patent on the "hanger." The company made a fortune and took credit for inventing one of the most-useful devices in modern history.

Parkhouse died penniless, but his shirts were wrinkle free.

WITHIN TWO YEARS OF ITS RELEASE,
OVER 100,000,000 SMILEY-FACE
BUTTONS WERE SOLD.

26 SMILEY FACE ICON

TAGLINE: A circle with two dots and a semicircle

PREDECESSOR: Fake cheerfulness without an easily identifiable symbol

LESSON: Be in the business of emotion, but don't be emotional about business.

In 1963, Richard Ball, co-owner of an advertising and PR firm in Worcester, Massachusetts, conceived the single most used and recognizable graphic icon of the past century—the smiley face.

Says its inventor: "I made a circle with a smile for a mouth on yellow paper, because it was sunshiny and bright. Turning the drawing upside down, the smile became a frown. Deciding that wouldn't do, I added two eyes." It took ten minutes.

Yep. That's it.

Did Ball do it to spread a message of peace? To promote tolerance and understanding? To spread joy among his fellow man?

No.

The icon was commissioned, and paid for, by an insurance company to help ease the bickering among its staff in the wake of a company merger. The insurance company ordered a "friendship campaign" and hired Ball to design an image for the buttons being passed out. And that was only the beginning.

In September 1970, the smiley face left the corporate world and hit the streets. Brothers Murray and Bernard Spain of Philadelphia set out to capitalize on the growing "hippie market," so they "borrowed" Ball's design. The two began manufacturing the smiley button for general consumption and, boy, did it take off. Within two years, more than one hundred million buttons were sold. And that simple smile continues to grace products and dot i's to this day.

So, yes, the graphic that we use to symbolize peace, joy, happiness, and bliss was the love child of two merging insurance companies that hated each other . . . until it was stolen and used to exploit hippies.

Have a nice day! ☺

"A rock pile ceases to be a rock pile the moment a single man contemplates it, bearing within him the image of a cathedral."

— ANTOINE DE SAINT-EXUPÉRY, *PILOTE DE GUERRE*

27 | PET ROCK

TAGLINE: A rock

PREDECESSOR: Real pets

LESSON: If there is no need, create one.

Maybe life was getting too complicated and people were subconsciously shunning technology. Maybe the first glimmer of the environmental movement was on the horizon, creating a desire to nurture Mother Earth. Or maybe the whole country was just high on those marijuana cigarettes. (It was, after all, the 1970s.) Who really knows?

One thing is certain: In 1975, a guy got *really* rich selling "domesticated" inanimate objects as pets. This despite the fact that you could easily capture and train "wild" rocks—for free. But who has that kind of time, right?

Advertising executive Gary Dahl conceived the Pet Rock in (where else but) California. Pet Rocks were simply stones that fit in the palm of your hand. That's it. They were purchased at a building supply store and sold as if they were pets.

The rocks, which sold for $3.95 each, came in a small cardboard "pet carrier" with their own wood shavings. A "Pet Rock Training Manual" was also provided to instruct idiots . . . um . . . pet owners on how to care and raise their new ward (though it did lack feeding instructions).

While the "sit" and "stay" commands covered in the manual were reliable, the "come" command was found to be extremely unsuccessful.

The fad lasted for all of six months, ending in Christmas of 1975. However, in those few months, the Pet Rock fetched its creator millions of dollars.

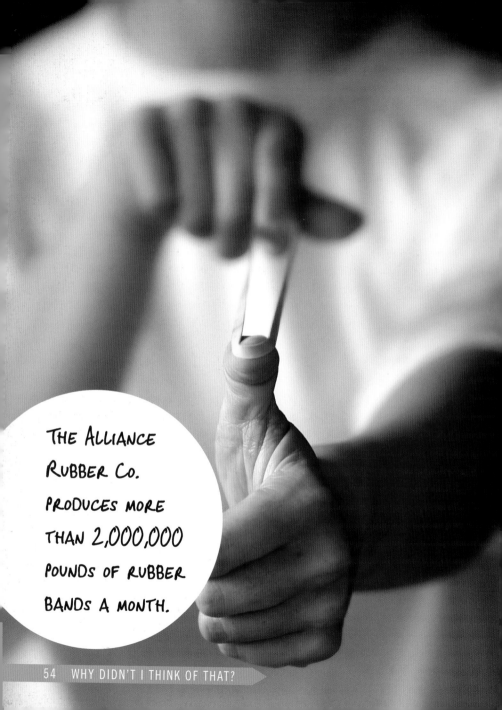

THE ALLIANCE
RUBBER CO.
PRODUCES MORE
THAN 2,000,000
POUNDS OF RUBBER
BANDS A MONTH.

28 | RUBBER BAND

TAGLINE: Stretchy little belt of rubber

PREDECESSOR: Boring, un-shootable string

LESSON: *Boing!*

While British inventor Stephen Perry patented the rubber band in 1845, it took a newspaper—and an American company—to really popularize the invention.

It's probably no surprise that a newspaper had a hand in popularizing the rubber band. But it's probably a surprise that it wasn't because the newspaper wrote about the product. Nope. The PR came from the paper using the band so its front-porch deliveries didn't blow all over the neighborhood.

On March 7, 1923, William H. Spencer of Alliance, Ohio, obtained rejected inner tubes from the Goodyear Tire & Rubber Company and began cutting them into bands in his basement. Spencer, who worked for the Pennsylvania Railroad, began trying to sell his rubber bands to office-supply stores and paper and twine outlets.

One day he noticed the *Akron Beacon Journal* blowing across his lawn and persuaded the *Beacon* to bind their papers with his bands. He talked the *Tulsa World* into doing the same, and persuaded grocers to use his rubber band instead of string to secure produce.

Spencer continued working for the railroad for fourteen years while building his rubber-band business. By 1944 he was able to open a second plant in Hot Springs, Arkansas. In 1957, he opened another in Franklin, Kentucky, and expanded to Salinas, California, in 1988. The Alliance Rubber Co. now produces more than two million pounds of rubber bands a month in addition to other office, mailing, and packaging products.

29 FRISBEE

TAGLINE: An upside-down plastic plate

PREDECESSOR: Projectiles with no whimsical floating abilities

LESSON: Find a new use for an old object.

It's 1947 . . . a Yale University student is looking for reasons to avoid studying. Suddenly, flying toward him in a graceful arc, like nothing he's seen before, is a cylindrical disk sailing effortlessly through the air. He picks it up and throws it back, and he's found the perfect excuse to procrastinate.

It all started with a baker named William Russel Frisbie who had been selling his pies to students at universities and schools in Connecticut and other parts of New England for some time. The students loved the pies and therefore had a lot of empty pie tins laying about with the words "FRISBIE'S PIES" emblazoned on them. College students are a resourceful bunch—I once personally saw a group of college students play a rousing game of baseball, for three hours, using a pinecone and a broom handle. The invention of the Frisbee took much less effort. Students started using the "Frisbie" pie pans in much the same way you see Frisbees used today. And it caught on, *big*!

In 1946, two partners, Walter Frederick Morrison and Warren Franscioni, caught wind of this phenomenon and pounced. They began to manufacture a plastic version of the device, which was much more aerodynamic and a lot more fun. The Morrison/Franscioni partnership did not last long though. Morrison went on to produce another version called the "Pluto Platter" hoping to cash in on the recent UFO craze and the nation's fascination with space. The Pluto Platter caught the eye of Richard Knerr and Arthur "Spud" Mellin at their new company Wham-O, which had just released the Hula Hoop (page 23) and the Super Ball (page 97). Upon hearing the story of the saucer's origins, Knerr changed the spelling of "Frisbie" and trademarked the flying disk. It's been known as the Frisbee ever since.

Today, more Frisbees are sold each year than footballs, baseballs, softballs, and soccer balls—combined.

And it all started with a procrastinator, a baker, and a Hula Hoop maker.

So *That's* Why They're Yellow (Part I)

It's an advertising trick from way back in the day. In the 1800s, China supplied the best graphite, and American pencil makers wanted their customers to know that their pencils contained it. That's why they painted them yellow (a color associated with royalty and respect in Chinese culture) and the rest is history.

30 | PENCIL

TAGLINE: The poor man's pen

PREDECESSOR: Charcoal

LESSON: The pencil is greater than the sword.

Think that's really lead in your pencil? Think again. While lead was originally used for the writing implement, it's been switched out for graphite. (Though most still refer to the core of a pencil as the lead.)

Graphite became a popular choice when a large quantity of it was discovered in England. While it left a better, darker mark than lead, the material was too soft to be used on its own. That's where the yellow casing we know and love today came into play. Pencil makers began hollowing out wooden sticks and inserting the graphite, creating a graphite-fueled writing implement that didn't break in your hand.

Stateside, cabinetmaker William Monroe of Concord, Massachusetts, was the first American to encase graphite in wood in 1812. Another early adopter was author Henry David Thoreau (yeah, that *Walden* guy). As far as manufacturers, Joseph Dixon's company (now Dixon Ticonderoga) began producing pencils en masse as did a number of factories established in New York and New Jersey, including Faber Castell, Berol, and General Pencil Company.

NECCO

NOW MAKES

750,000,000

CANDY DOTS

A YEAR.

31 CANDY DOTS

TAGLINE: A sugar high complete with a choking hazard

PREDECESSOR: Blobs of sugar without paper attached

LESSON: People love anything made of blobs of sugar.

Depending on how old you are, you may remember going to the candy store as a child to get these long strips of what looked like adding machine paper (and depending on how old you are, you may actually remember adding machine paper). Dozens of little sugar dots were glued to the paper and you cheerfully nibbled them off, later choking on the paper that was inevitably still attached to each one.

Candy dots, the nostalgic sugary sensation, also known as "paper candy" or "candy buttons," were originally introduced by the Cumberland Valley Company. Engineer and inventor George Theofiel Dib invented the candy button machine that produces this confectionary wonder. NECCO acquired the brand in 1980. NECCO now makes seven hundred fifty million candy dots a year.

These dots are an inexpensive way to remember what it was like to be a kid. Picking the tiny little candies off with your teeth, little bits of paper accumulating in the back of your throat, inevitably making you gag and vomit a rainbow of sugary fun all over the neighbor's driveway. Good times. Good times.

They're Flavored?

There are three flavors on each paper strip:

- Cherry (pink)
- Lime (blue)
- Lemon (yellow)

Though they all just taste like blobs of sugar.

32 | THE GAME OF JACKS

TAGLINE: Plucking many mini metal stars between ball bounces

PREDECESSOR: Finding something else to do

LESSON: Kids will play with just about anything.

I wasn't a big jacks player back in my day. I suppose most guys weren't. And the game was a lot more popular back in the '50s and '60s when, depending upon whom you ask, times were simpler and so were games. Now there's probably an electronic version. (I just Googled it and, yes, there is.)

When I was a boy, I remember my mother showing me how to play. She was very good, which makes me 150 years old. My mom taught me all she knew about playing jacks and before I knew it I was swiping fivesies with the best of them.

This game of quick reflexes actually dates back much further than the '50s. Although back then, players weren't snatching up jacks made of metal, instead they were swiping at everything from pebbles and clay to wood and ivory to small bones and Brontosaurus teeth.*

When the game first arrived in America, it was called jack-stones or five-stones, as it was played with five stones and no ball. As the game evolved, one of the jacks was swapped out for a wooden ball, and a rubber ball later replaced that. The last step in its evolution was switching the jacks from stones to the small, metal star-like pieces we are familiar with today. These are reminiscent of the original animal knucklebones used.

Repulsive? Sure, but still . . . a very simple concept that made game-makers a fortune and is still popular today!

 Okay, so maybe not Brontosaurus teeth.

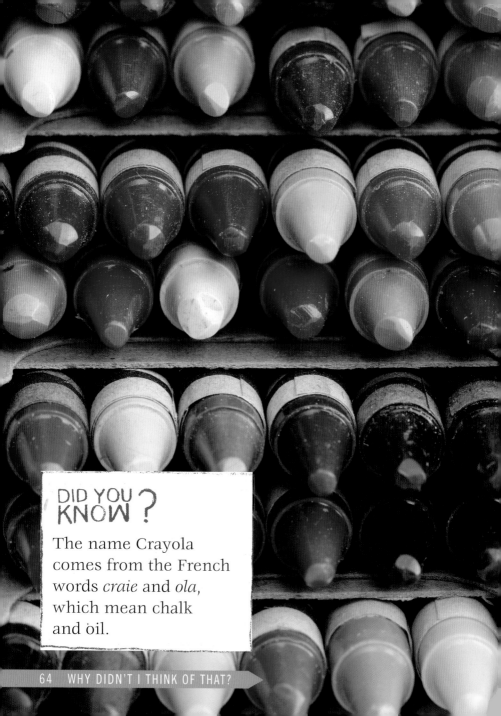

DID YOU KNOW?

The name Crayola comes from the French words *craie* and *ola*, which mean chalk and oil.

33 CRAYONS

TAGLINE: Waxy coloring sticks

PREDECESSOR: Paint

LESSON: Encourage creativity in kids.

According to Crayola, "Today, the world is a very colorful place. But it wasn't always that way." Let's face it, Crayola, the world has *always* been a very colorful place—unless of course you're colorblind, in which case, trust me, it is. But I digress.

Before Crayola was Crayola it was Binney & Smith, a manufacturer of industrial colorants. Among its many accomplishments before helping kids learn to color inside the lines were two staples in Americana: the bright red barn and the black automobile tire. The black dye added to the Goodrich Company's white rubber tires gave them their black color as well as made them more durable; the red pigment used in the barn paint helped the live-stock stable become the measure for which people can or cannot hit things. But I digress, again—back to the crayon at hand.

Today there are a number of different companies that offer crayon sets. Yet the most recognized name in the world of crayons is still Crayola. According to the Binney & Smith website, the Crayola brand has 99 percent name recognition among consumers in the United States, and, as if that's not enough, the company is looking to build that recognition by selling Crayola products in eighty different countries. The crayon king has come out with over 100 different colors and a number of specialty packs, yet one question still remains: What the hell is that white one for?

The Original Eight
In 1903 the first pack of Crayola crayons came with eight colors. They were:

Black	Violet
Blue	Orange
Brown	Yellow
Red	Green

IT WASN'T UNTIL 1960
THAT THE FIRST AUTO CUP
HOLDERS WERE TESTED.

34 | AUTOMOBILE CUP HOLDER

TAGLINE: A hole

PREDECESSOR: The groin

LESSON: The simpler, the better.

Like many of the items featured in this book, the cup holder has become so common, it hardly seems like an invention at all. It's as if the automobile cup holder has been around forever, like the sun or Larry King. Yet, it's a relatively recent invention.

You'd think someone would have thought of this immediately after man began riding on stuff. However, it wasn't until 1960 that the first auto cup holders were tested, but they didn't even catch on then. Remember, in the 1960s, seatbelts (page 125) weren't standard features in automobiles, and child car seats weren't even on the horizon. When you're busy worrying about you and your kids flying from your vehicle, I guess your beverage isn't *that* big of a priority. But once seatbelts and car seats became common, people began turning their attention to the safety of their Slurpies. Built-in cup holders began to be widely available in the 1980s, coming standard in many minivans.

Then, as is often the case with well-known inventions, timing played a pivotal role in securing the cup holder's place in the American car market. Out of nowhere came Stella Liebeck, a seventy-nine-year-old from Albuquerque, New Mexico. Stella ordered a cup of coffee from the local McDonald's drive-thru and promptly spilled it on herself. She suffered third-degree burns and sued Ronald and Company for $2.9 million. Incredibly, she won.

Realizing Stella could have just as easily sued the car company, automobile manufacturers redoubled their efforts to provide ample cup holders in all their new vehicles from that point on.

Stella, you feisty old bird, I think I speak for fluid-consuming motorists everywhere when I say, "Thank you."

35 SOCCER

TAGLINE: Twenty-two people trying to kick a ball into a net during a riot

PREDECESSOR: Less emotional ball kicking

LESSON: Boredom is the stepmother of invention.

The game of soccer can be traced back to a number of different ancient cultures (surprisingly, none of them Brazilian). The Romans, Greeks, Chinese, and medieval Europeans can all stake a claim to the ball-in-net pastime. Archeological evidence proves a game with similar construct was played way back when by the multi-deity-fearing Romans and Greeks. Putting a military spin on the sport of Pelé, soldiers in Han Dynasty China built their skills by kicking a ball into a net. But it took the medieval Europeans to give us the riot-inciting game we* love today.

Way before Man. U versus Liverpool, medieval villages squared off in soccer-like matches and started bitter rivalries with each other. As in today's version, kicking, punching, biting, and gouging were allowed. Hundreds of townspeople came out en masse to take part in the games and accompanying hooliganism, which could go on for hours upon hours—even up to a whole day. There are even rumors that a decapitated human head was sometimes used as the ball. These matches and rivalries proved so violent that the government tried to ban the sport completely.

In 1333, England's King Edward III passed a number of laws in an attempt to stop the soccer madness. Scotland's King James I followed Edward's lead in 1424 by decrying, "That na man play at the Fute-ball!" This loosely translates to: "Enough with the %*#!-ing soccer already."

It didn't work.

Today soccer is the most popular sport in the world.

 By "we," I mean all countries outside of the United States, where the MLS is on par with the WNBA and major league shuffleboard.

THE DIXIE CUP COMPANY MERGED WITH THE AMERICAN CAN COMPANY IN 1957 FORMING A BEVERAGE-HOLDER SUPER-GROUP. THE SUPER-GROUP IS NOW IN THE FOLD OF KOCH INDUSTRIES, THE UNITED STATES' LARGEST PRIVATELY OWNED COMPANY!

36 PAPER CUP

TAGLINE: Cups you chuck

PREDECESSOR: The no-chuck cup

LESSON: Convenience is king.

"Death in School Drinking Cups!" was the title of a study by Alvin Davison, a Lafayette College biology professor. The study was published in the August 1908 issue of *Technical World Magazine*, and was based on research done in the Pennsylvania public schools.

Davison was so alarmed because during the early twentieth century, it was common to have shared cups or dippers at public water sources. As you can imagine, the sharing made people sick. Everybody was diving into the same stagnant pools like a bunch of hogs at a trough!

Luckily, Davison's study came out the same year as the Dixie Cup was invented. So his call for alarm paired with the availability of disposable cups, resulted in the passage of many laws ending the use of shared drinking cups in public schools.

It took a little longer for hospitals to catch on to the paper-cup craze. It wasn't until 1942 that Massachusetts State College published a study exposing the high-cost of sanitizing glassware for reuse in hospitals. As it turned out, the cost of reusing glasses was nearly two times as high as using the disposable alternative. A loss for Mother Nature, but a win for people going into the hospital and not leaving dead.

The Dixie Cup company took full advantage of this new trend and instantly began making millions.

A 1957 merger with the American Can Company saw the formation of a beverage-holder super-group. The super-group is now in the fold of Koch Industries, the United States' largest privately owned company.

CHESTER GREENWOOD &
COMPANY PRODUCED 400,000
PAIRS OF EARMUFFS IN 1936.

37 EARMUFFS

TAGLINE: Cold weather cover-ups

PREDECESSOR: Cold ears

LESSON: What's good for your ears might be good for everybody's ears.

Where else would this invention start but with cold ears? This particular set of ears belonged to Chester Greenwood, a fifteen-year-old with an inventive spirit and a bitter hatred of the bitter cold.

As reported in the *Wall Street Journal*, "Chester Greenwood's ears were so sensitive that they turned chalky white, beet red, and deep blue (in that order) when the mercury dipped." But you can't believe everything you read (except in this book, of course). I think it's more likely that Chester was sort of a wuss. Most kids would simply put a hat on to solve the problem, but little Chester's ears were sensitive to wool.

So, one day in 1873 Chester decided to do something nerdy about it. He approached his grandmother for advice and help in creating an effective ear-shielding device. I imagine their conversation went something like this . . .

Chester: *Hey Grannndmaaa!* What big cold ears I have!
Grandmother: The better to make millions of dollars with my dear!

He called their collaborative effort the Greenwood Champion Ear Protector. And it didn't take Chester too long to create. It was extremely simple—some bent wire, a little insulating material, and some sewing. He founded the Chester Greenwood & Company in order to manufacture and sell his invention. According to the official website of the state of Maine, his company had its biggest year in 1936 when it produced 400,000 pairs of earmuffs.

The Ear Protector, or "muff," was an instant hit. And it's all because Chester had cold, itchy ears.

2,000,000,000 POUNDS OF CHOCOLATE ARE PRODUCED EACH YEAR.

DID YOU KNOW?

The Snickers bar is the bestselling candy bar in the world, with annual global sales of $2 billion.

38 CANDY BAR

TAGLINE: Candy in the shape of a bar

PREDECESSOR: Smaller pieces of candy

LESSON: Sometimes a lot of people can make a lot of money from one idea.

Before being messily killed by Spanish invaders, Aztec Emperor Montezuma loved sipping on his favorite chocolate drink made from *cacao*. Conquistador Hernando Cortez, the man behind Montezuma's killing, brought the drink to Spain in 1529. It became an instant favorite of the Spanish royalty, and later spread to the rest of Europe where it became equally popular. It took three centuries on the continent before it was turned into a solid confection.

In 1847, the English company Joseph Fry & Son discovered a way to mix a chocolate-drink-based concoction into a paste that could be pressed into a mold. And *voilà!* The chocolate bar was born!

Soon people began eating chocolate as much as drinking it. John Cadbury began selling a similar version of the Joseph Fry & Son chocolate bar in 1849. However, the early bars of chocolate were bittersweet. To solve this problem, Henri Nestlé (of *the* Nestlé chocolate company) and Daniel Peter introduced milk chocolate in 1875.

All of this caught the eye of Milton S. Hershey, already a caramel tycoon (I swear). Seeing the potential, Hershey installed chocolate machinery in his Lancaster factory, and ended up producing his first chocolate bars in 1900.

Today, 2 billion pounds of chocolate are produced each year. And believe it or not, the United States doesn't take top honor in its consumption. According to WeAreSweet.com, the Swiss consume the most chocolate.

By 1856,
Saratoga Springs
was producing
nearly 7,000,000
bottles per
year.

39 | BOTTLED WATER

TAGLINE: Free water that you buy

PREDECESSOR: Free water

LESSON: There's no such thing as a stupid idea, and *sell free stuff*.

It might be easier (and funnier) to dismiss bottled water as a brilliant marketing ploy, but there was actually a real need that fueled the industry. Seems some people didn't like dying gruesome deaths from cholera, E. coli, and other diseases. Pansies.

Even as early as the dawn of the Roman Empire, spring water was being routed into the city of Rome from miles away by aqueducts. In fact, the thirst for spring water is older than the United States. Water was being bottled in Boston as early as 1767. (Of course they mixed it with some other stuff and called it beer.) But seriously, folks, bottled water became a serious money-making industry once glass bottling made the process more cost-efficient. By 1856, Saratoga Springs was producing nearly seven million bottles per year. It became a booming industry.

The boom subsided a little when municipalities started adding chlorine to public drinking water (*mmm!* chlorine), taking away the health risk associated with filling your glass at the tap. However, there was a second bottled-water boom in 1977 thanks to Perrier's yuppie-targeted marketing. The $5 million campaign made bottled water as essential in yuppie culture as the BMW. And as Dr. Francis H. Chapelle notes in his book *Wellsprings: A Natural History of Bottled Spring Waters*, Perrier "was all the things yuppies wanted in a lifestyle-defining product."

These days, Americans consume the most bottled water in the world, despite the fact that nearly every person in the United States has access to perfectly safe drinking water.

DID YOU KNOW ?

Campylobacteriosis is a bacterial disease that can infect humans through contact with dog feces. It causes mild to severe nausea—and all the good things that go along with that. The Center for Disease Control advises pet owners to wash their hands after handling poop in order to avoid this and other bacterial diseases.

40 POOPER SCOOPER

TAGLINE: A scoop for picking up poop

PREDECESSOR: Just walking away

LESSON: Don't be shy. Give it a try . . . if for no other reason than *E. coli*.

It's not just a matter of getting it on your shoe, or even one of common courtesy. It's a health thing. As a leading source of E. coli, your pup's poop is full of bacterial coliforms (no not *Colorforms*—those delightful, vinyl-based children's toys—*coliforms*). Sure, one dog's waste might not cause global chaos and illness, but a city's worth of pets pooping in the streets every which way to Sunday would create a serious health hazard. Makes you really want to clean up after your mutt.

According to the website InventionConnection.com, Brooke Miller, of Anaheim, California, is the one who helped dog owners do just that by inventing the pooper scooper. Her original design, for which she holds the patent, is a receptacle attached to a wooden stick, with a small rake for people to use to gather the waste into the bin. It's not known for sure when Miller invented the pooper scooper, but according to InvenionConnection.com, the term was included in dictionaries in the early 1970s.

Today, nearly every urban, suburban, and rural area in the United States has made it illegal to leave your dog's poop behind in public.

> "To invent, you need a good imagination and a pile of junk."
>
> **—THOMAS A. EDISON**

Heat + Oxygen + Fuel These are the three ingredients to a fire, as identified by firefighting professionals. If you remove one of the ingredients, out goes the fire.

41 FIRE

TAGLINE: Fire

PREDECESSOR: Cold

LESSON: Cold bad. Fire goooood.

While fire may technically be more of a discovery than an invention, this book would be incomplete without its inclusion. It is thought that the discovery of fire most likely happened when a lightning strike ignited a tree or some brush during prehistoric times, though it's impossible to say exactly how it came about. I'd like to think it went a little something like this . . .

> **Grog:** Light from sky make tree burn!
> **Steve:** Fire burn squirrel in tree.
> **Grog:** Me eat squirrel. Pass salt.
> **Steve:** Salt not been discovered yet.
> **Grog:** *Grrr!*

It's believed that the controlled use of fire started during the Early Stone Age. Some of the earliest evidence of Grog and pals getting their barbecue on was discovered at an archaeological dig site in Benot Ya'aqov, Israel, where charred seeds and a You Kiss Cook Now! apron* were uncovered, dating back 790,000 years.

Controlled fire is arguably man's most significant discovery, pertinent for warmth, illumination, and, of course, adequately describing the pants of a liar-liar.

> "Human subtlety [. . .] will never devise an invention more beautiful, more simple or more direct than does nature, because in her inventions nothing is lacking, and nothing is superfluous."
>
> **—LEONARDO DA VINCI**

✱ I made that up.

DID YOU KNOW ?

In the United States, there was a three-month ban on sliced bread during World War II.

42 SLICED BREAD

Sometimes the best inventions are ways to slice other inventions into smaller pieces. Wait . . . that didn't come out right. What I mean is, sometimes the best inventions are *modifications* of other inventions. That's better. In this case, we're talking about modifying an invention that has, literally, fed the world for centuries—bread.

Ottis Frederick Rohwedder came up with the idea in 1917. And it only took him seventeen years to sell it. In addition to some personal and business problems, Ottis had to overcome the doubts of bread-makers who were uncertain that people would want to buy pre-sliced bread. They rightfully surmised that the loaves would get stale quicker that way. Ottis solved this problem by packaging the bread immediately after slicing it. In 1928, sliced bread began its rapid climb toward being the norm.

So why has sliced bread become the standard to which all other inventions are held? Is it because it added a level of convenience to a product that was such a staple in the world's diet? Is it because it arrived at a time in our history when timesaving was at a premium? Nope.

In 1930, Wonder Bread coined the saying, "The greatest thing since sliced bread" in an advertising campaign. The slogan stuck and has become a way to applaud an invention. Makes you wonder how they described Ottis's first loaf.

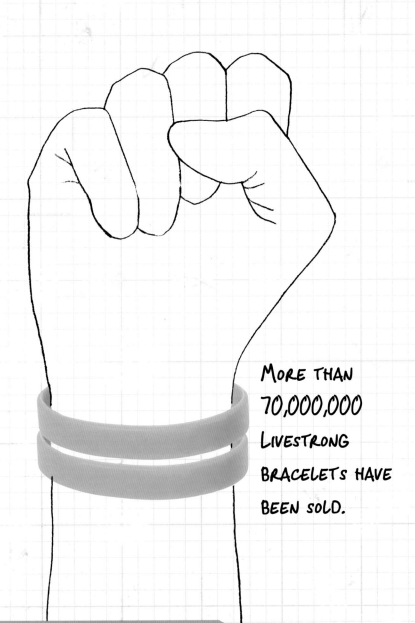

MORE THAN
70,000,000
LIVESTRONG
BRACELETS HAVE
BEEN SOLD.

43 AWARENESS BRACELETS

TAGLINE: Rubber bands

PREDECESSOR: Awareness ribbons

LESSON: Charity is good, but let's not get carried away.

It all started with cyclist Lance Armstrong. Remember that little yellow wristband everybody was wearing a few years back? It was meant to raise awareness for the Lance Armstrong Foundation's Live Strong campaign, which began after he beat cancer and then the competition at the Tour De France, something like ninety times. Manufactured by Nike, its sales went to cancer research and helped raise awareness while delivering the message: Live life to the fullest. And, well, people went nuts for the thing.

The goal of this particular awareness bracelet was to raise $25 million. It made that goal in six months. Since the effort started in 2004, more than seventy million Livestrong bracelets have been sold, and sales are still, well, *strong*.

> ### So *That's* Why They're Yellow (Part II)
> The wristband's yellow because of the color's importance in cycling. During the Tour de France and other cycling competitions, the overall leader wears a yellow jersey.

As expected, other charities (actually, practically *all* of them) followed this fundraising trend. It seems like just about every other charity adopted an awareness bracelet specific to its cause, 'cause of the Livestrong success and peer pressure.

DID YOU KNOW ?

Any instrument that is
played by beating on
a membrane stretched
across a hollowed
out body is called a
membranophone.

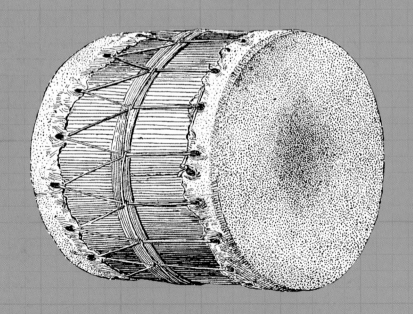

44 DRUM

TAGLINE: Anything upon which one bangs

PREDECESSOR: Clapping

LESSON: Tap into an industry that's booming.

The concept of the drum is as old (and annoying) as humans banging their hands on any hard surface. It seems we as a species have an inherent need to make noise in order to attract attention to ourselves. So there's really no one person who invented the concept of "drumming"; however, the drum as we know it has evolved quite a bit.

As you can tell, there's a difference between drumming on the ground and drumming on something that's been hollowed out, like a log, a gourd, or my head. The idea of using empty space to amplify sound is the basis behind the membranophone—any instrument that is played by beating on a membrane stretched across a hollowed out body. It's presumed the original membranophone was built from a hollow stump with an animal skin stretched over it. A little different than the Pearl gathering dust in your basement, but structurally it's the same idea.

Today, drums are made from a variety of materials. The idea of the "drum set" has also changed. Rather than a stump and a couple of gourds, the modern drum set typically includes a bass drum, a snare drum, tom-toms, a floor tom, and a cymbal (with the option to go overboard and add more variations to your kit).

But while the construction has changed over time, the purpose remains the same. The drum is a means of communication. It's used in just about every musical genre from rock to hip-hop and has cultural variations like the Cuban bongo and African conga.

DID YOU KNOW?

Using a straw when drinking a sugary beverage helps reduce tooth decay.

45 | STRAW

TAGLINE: Plumbing for your mouth

PREDECESSOR: Suctionless drinking

LESSON: Let's face it. Sometimes the best inventions suck.

The earliest drinking straws were made from hollowed out pieces of grass and reed. Figure out how the invention got its name?

In 1888, Marvin C. Stone sought to improve on the natural straw by patenting the paper straw. However, this "improvement" was actually inferior. Why? It was made of an absorbent material. A little detrimental if you're hoping to have liquid travel through it. Every sip a person took damaged the straw. Inefficient and wasteful—so it was back to the drawing board.

It was a combination of Stone's patent and nonabsorbent plastic that got us to the effective device we use today. But the brainstorming didn't stop there. Now that the straw could actually be used, inventors had a field day with the different types of straws that could be created. Stone's paper straw bore:

- The bendable straw, with its flexible neck
- The crazy straw, with tons of twists and turns for your drink to take
- The spoon straw, perfect for scooping the last bit of slush or milkshake
- The mini-straw, which comes attached to your favorite juicebox
- The edible straw, made out of food like candy and cookies and cereal

There were a few dips in the process, but the straw has come a long way from the piece of grass it once was.

Animal Crackers by the Numbers

- Varieties of animals used: 37
- Current number of species: 17
- Number of crackers per box: 22
- Amount of string used per year: 6,000 miles
- Number of cookies made per minute: 12,000
- Number of packages sold in a year: 40,000,000

46 ANIMAL CRACKERS

TAGLINE: Cookies disguised as crackers disguised as animals

PREDECESSOR: Round, vegetarian-friendly treats

LESSON: Make a kid feel like a giant and you will make yourself a giant sum of cash.

Bears and bison and camels and cougars and elephants and giraffes and gorillas and hippopotami and hyenas and kangaroos and lions and monkeys and rhinoceros and seals and sheep and tigers and zebras . . . oh my! These are the seventeen types of animals trapped in cookie-form as today's Animal Crackers.

In the 1800s, sweet "toothes" on both sides of the Atlantic enjoyed biting the heads off little baked beasts. However, it took snack food powerhouse National Biscuit Company (now known as Nabisco) teaming up with show-biz pioneer PT Barnum for the Animal Crackers we know and love today to be introduced. Packaged in a box made to look like a circus car, Barnum's Animal Crackers were rolled out in 1902 at five cents a pop.

A hit from the get-go, the partnership between the company that brought us the Oreo and the man who coined the phrase "There's a sucker born every minute" was a financial success. While the shapes may have changed (thirty-seven animals have been used) and the price has gone up, Animal Crackers are still popular today. Shipped out to seventeen countries, an estimated forty million boxes are sold each year. (Even at the original nickel apiece, that's some serious cookie dough.)

Despite the fact that they're nothing fancy, Animal Crackers keep snackers coming back for more . . . I figure it's because they like to bite the heads off. Me? I like to bite the heads off.

FISHING IS A $40,000,000,000 INDUSTRY IN THE UNITED STATES.

47 FISHING ROD

TAGLINE: A stick, string, and hook attached to a guy with wishes of gullible fishes

PREDECESSOR: Less suspicious fishes (say *that* ten times fast)

LESSON: Give a man a fish; you have fed him for a day. Teach a man to fish; you can sell him fishing equipment and beer.

Sure, fishermen way back when had nets and spears to help in their maritime hunt—but those methods, along with trying to snag a fish with your bare hands, required *you* to go to the *fish*. The invention of the fishing rod brought the lazy man's logic to this process. Why go to the fish when the fish could come to you? Brilliant!

Judging by the ancient "Gone Fishing" signs found hanging from doors of prehistoric ruins, the bring-the-fish-to-me mentality spread throughout the old world. Artifacts of angling—the British term for fishing—have been found in Egypt, China, Greece, and Italy, as well as England, proving medieval Englishmen knew a thing or two about catching fish even before the deep fryer was invented.

Modern rods may have a few minor differences from the ones back then (such as the use of graphite poles rather than sticks), but the concept has stayed the same. It's the most convenient and efficient way for a person to gather fish. So man has remained fed and happy due to his ingenuity, while fish, on the other hand, have remained pissed off ever since.

Aside from the fact that the fishing rod has helped to feed billions of people since its invention, it's helped to make man a boatload of money. In the United States alone, fishing is a $40 *billion* industry. Looking for that next big idea? Go fish.

DID YOU KNOW?

The study of bells is called campanology.

48 BELL

TAGLINE: A great gong that goes *ding, dong*

PREDECESSOR: Not gonging

LESSON: Make making music simple.

Ringing a bell—what could be a simpler way to make music? (Okay, by its inclusion in this book, "banging a drum" would be an appropriate response.)

Like a drum, a bell can be made from just about anything. Some are clay, some are wood, but most modern bells are usually metal. In terms of where it hangs in the musical family, the bell is classified as a percussion instrument. And while its simplicity makes it nearly impossible to identify when exactly the first bell was rung, we do know that it is one of the oldest musical instruments ever invented. Bells are depicted in stone tablets and other carvings that date to the fourth century B.C.

Whether they are used as part of religious rites or as a mere decorative piece on a mantel, one thing is for sure: Bells are, have been, and always will be a huge part of human culture. And the bell proves you don't need all sorts of bells and whistles to create a sound invention.

Famous Bells

Believe it or not, there are some pretty famous bells around the world. Here's the rundown on five important ones:

- The Liberty Bell—located in Philadelphia, Pennsylvania, it's a symbol of American freedom, having been rung on July 4, 1776
- Big Ben—it's the bell inside the Great Clock in the Clock Tower at the Palace of Westminster, one of the most recognizable structures in the world
- The World Peace Bell—located in Newport, Kentucky, it's the largest swinging bell in existence
- The Great Mingun Bell—the largest functioning bell in existence (at 90 tons), it's found in Myanmar
- The Tsar Bell—the largest bell still in existence, it's on display in Moscow

WHAM-O'S SUPER BALL SOLD OVER 7,000,000 UNITS IN ITS FIRST SIX MONTHS OF RELEASE.

49 SUPER BALLS

Like many of the inventions in this book, the Super Ball took an existing technology to new heights, literally. The chemistry behind the creation of rubber is complicated. The story behind the Super Ball, however, is simple . . . and a little weird.

During his spare time, California chemist Norman Stingley decided for whatever reason to compress some rubber under 3,500 pounds of pressure. (Because that's what chemists do for fun, I guess.) And thus Stingley succeeded in creating a ball with unprecedented bouncy-ness.

Then came Wham-O, once again, to the rescue. By then, Wham-O was adept at marketing wacky things, like the Frisbee, the Slip 'N Slide, and the Hula Hoop. With the toy company's big promotional bounce, Super Balls caught on with a *boing*.

Launched in 1965, the Super Ball became every child's favorite plaything, selling over seven million units in its first six months of release. At ninety-eight cents apiece, that's gross sales of $6.8 million, which roughly translates to $463 million today.

The Wham-O Super Ball, and other generic super-bouncy balls, continue to be a favorite for kids around the world.

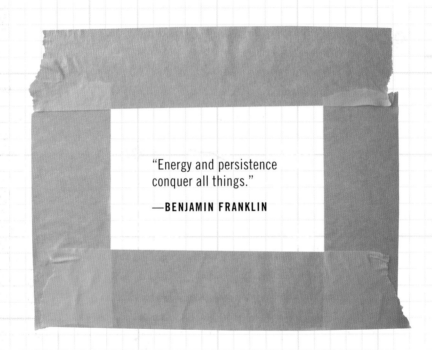

"Energy and persistence conquer all things."

—**BENJAMIN FRANKLIN**

50 MASKING TAPE

TAGLINE: A painter's best friend

PREDECESSOR: Stickier tape and butcher paper

LESSON: Trust hard-working employees with initiative.

The 3M Company is mentioned several times in this book, and it seems like the story is always the same. It goes something like this:

> **Innovative 3M Employee:** Hey! I've got this great idea for a new product!
>
> **3M Manager:** *Get back to work on that other sticky thing.*
>
> **Innovative 3M Employee:** Look!
>
> **3M Manager:** *Get back to work on that other sticky thing.*
>
> **Innovative 3M Employee:** You sure about that, boss?
>
> **3M Manager:** Ah . . . maybe you're right. Let's make billions of dollars off your idea. *Now get back to work on that other sticky thing.*

And such was the case with masking tape.

One afternoon 3M employee Dick Drew went to an auto-repair shop to test some new sandpaper he was working on. But rather than get feedback on the sandpaper, he received an earful about painting. It seems the mechanics could no longer deal with the tape and butcher-paper combo that was used for two-tone paint jobs. It just didn't cut it. In their frustration, Drew saw opportunity. He returned to his 3M lab determined to help those men out. He set out to create a butcher-paper/tape hybrid that would solve their coverage issue. And he did just that. But not before he got in trouble with then-company-president William McKnight. It seems McKnight didn't want Drew spending time on such a project. Though lucky for him, 3M, and us, Drew didn't listen. He kept at it and invented masking tape, a sort of sticky-paper that could be used to block off areas a painter didn't want to paint. (Of course people found other uses for the tape as well.)

Goes to show—even if it gets sticky at times, it's best to persevere.

THE THUMBTACK IS ONE OF THE TOP-SELLING
OFFICE PRODUCTS OF ALL TIME.

51 THUMBTACK

TAGLINE: A miniature nail

PREDECESSOR: The nail

LESSON: Make a "light" version of something that's already useful.

The modern thumbtack was derived from Edwin Moore's map pin. (Map pin? Ever gone on a website to get directions and used those virtual push-pins to determine your location? Those, except real.) In 1900, Moore founded the Moore Push-Pin Company with $112.60, and as the founder and only employee, Moore spent all his time laboriously producing these pointy push-pins. The first sale was for one gross, or twelve dozen, that brought in $2. Orders only went up from there though as the Eastman Kodak Company soon placed one for $1,000 (approximately $25,000 nowadays). The company used Moore's invention to "tack" up their photographs.

And that brings us to how Moore's map pushpin evolved into the thumbtack. In 1903, a few years after Moore founded the Moore Push-Pin Company, German clockmaker Johann Kirsten designed the first thumbtack. Similar in construction, Kirsten's thumbtack had a flat head opposite the point, whereas Moore's pushpin had a tiny grip of sorts.

Besides the flathead versus grip difference, the two men also went in different directions with their lives post-creation of the pointy inventions. Moore went on to invent and patent a number of other items, including the picture hanger. (Guess he had a hang-up for hanging stuff up.) Kirsten on the other hand sold the rights to his invention to Otto Lindstedt, who patented it in 1904. Lindstedt became very wealthy. Kirsten remained broke. Not too sharp—the thumbtack remains one of the top-selling office products of all time.

Top 5 Tambourine-ists of All Time
1. Tracy Partridge
2. Stevie Nicks
3. Davy Jones
4. Roger Daltry
5. Anyone who picks up the instrument

52 | TAMBOURINE

TAGLINE: A one-hand band

PREDECESSOR: A less annoying Salvation Army

LESSON: People love jingly things.

One part opened-bottomed drum and one-part bells, it's little more than a child's toy. Yet it has played a part in popular music for more than 3,000 years.

All the "musician" (and I use the term loosely) has to do is tap the tambourine to create a combination drum-and-jingle sound. Playing the instrument really requires little more than giving it a clap. (Not *the* clap, *a* clap— just wanna make that clear for all those musicians out there . . . . Musicians spreading music with a clap, great; musicians spreading the clap, with music, not so great.)

> ### "Honey, Would You Pick Me Up Some Tympanons?"
> Small drums like the tambourine called *tympanons* were used in ancient Rome, Greece, and Mesopotamia. For some reason, there was always an argument when women asked their husbands to pick some up at the marketplace.

Today the tambourine is played just about anywhere there is music. Of course, the instrument's biggest claim to fame came when Tracy Partridge (the little mute girl) played it so skillfully on *The Partridge Family*. And what would "Come on Get Happy" be without that mean drum-and-jingle?

53 | PLASTIC MILK CRATE

TAGLINE: Furniture for college students

PREDECESSOR: Wooden crates

LESSON: Useful objects may have other uses—think ahead and capitalize on them.

The story of the milk crate isn't so much one of invention but of *re*invention. As is often the case with a good idea, the milk crate was created to do one thing but ended up becoming popular for quite another.

Obviously, the milk crate was invented to transport milk. And originally, it was crafted out of wood or metal. However, the '60s brought about the plastic crate, and its rise in nondairy–related uses. From functioning as shelves to bed-raisers to stools, milk crates became the go-to home furnishing for the young-and-broke. Its new use as the perfect piece of flexible furniture caused not only a rise in its popularity but also in the rate at which it was swiped.

Until recently, the majority of the pilfering was blamed on college students who use milk crates to construct just about every piece of furniture one can imagine. Recently though, it has been discovered that milk crates are being stolen by actual thieves, ground up, sent to China, and used in the creation of a wide variety of goods. Yeah, apparently there's a milk crate mafia! Because of this, dairies now often hire private investigators to rout out the milk crate marauders. Think that's a little excessive? Milk crate thefts cost dairies millions of dollars per year.

So the next time you try to pinch a milk crate from a back alley, remember: Somebody's got to pay for it. And if you're snagged by a Land-O-Lakes private Dick, it might just be you.

Factory Fact
The Union Paper Bag Machine Company is still in operation. Though now, International Paper runs the plant.

54 PAPER BAG

TAGLINE: A disposable sack

PREDECESSOR: Bringing a nondisposable bag with you (Heaven forbid!)

LESSON: Today, disposable items are no longer an option. Create an item that does the same thing without harming the environment. Good luck with that.

Imagine a time long ago when people took their own canvas bags to the grocery store to carry home their booty . . . what's that? The time "long ago" was last Sunday? Oh, right. Well, imagine it's a few years ago—before Al Gore and his *Inconvenient Truth*—*now* imagine a time long ago when people took their own canvas bags to the grocery store to carry home their booty. An outrageous idea, yeah? Why would someone bring his own bags when there are all those paper bags to use? The paper bag was the way to transport your milk, produce, and other purchases before it became environmentally uncool to do so. And before that happened, a couple of people managed to make some serious scratch off the paper bag.

The first person to do so was Francis Wolle. He is credited with recognizing the need for a disposable bag and filling it. Not only did he invent the paper bag, he invented the machine that mass-produced these throwaway carriers. And in 1869, he founded the Union Paper Bag Machine Company with his brother and other partners looking to cash in on the paper bag craze. (Okay, maybe "craze" is a bit of an overkill—but it was damned exciting for Wolle and his posse.)

However, Wolle's bags aren't the kind you see today in shopping marts and malls. No, the square-bottomed bag you see in stores today was invented by Margaret Knight. You could say inventing was her "bag" as she's the noted inventor of ninety creations and holds twenty-two patents. But it's the square-bottomed bag that's her real claim to fame.

Knight went on to make millions from the invention, and her product is still used to this day (take that Al Gore). Now *that's* a bag lady!

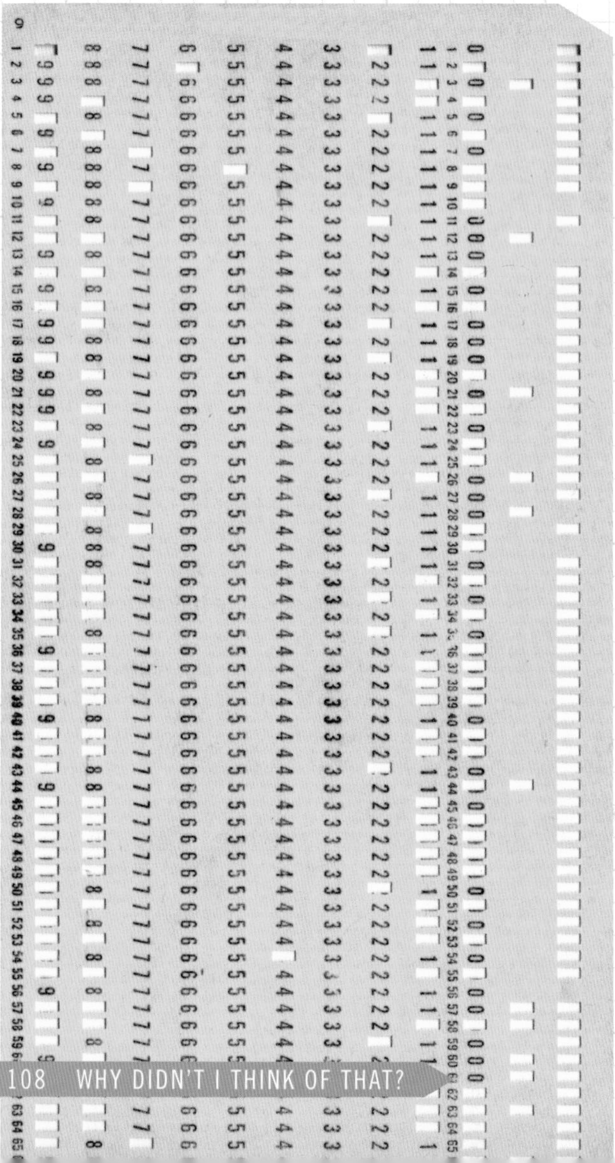

55 | COMPUTER PUNCH CARD

TAGLINE: A card with holes in it

PREDECESSOR: The abacus

LESSON: Today's "okay" invention can revolutionize tomorrow's world.

Computers are great. Wait . . . I'm really understating that. Computers are amazing and have radically transformed modern civilization more than any invention *ever* (even if Hollywood's right and they one day enslave mankind in a nightmarish post-apocalyptic hell). Honestly remarkable. However, none of that would be possible if it weren't for one thing: the punch card.

The evolution from 9" × 4" paper card to 3.0GHz computer processor is a complicated one. Lucky for you (and me), we're concerned about the simple things in this book. And the simple thing in this evolutionary tract is the punch card—a truly revolutionary yet straightforward invention. Here's a brief timeline of this hole-y creation:

- 1725: Punch cards are first used to control textile looms in France.
- 1832: Semen Korsakov uses the punch card to store information for the statistics department of the Russian Police Ministry.
- 1837: Charles Babbage begins theorizing about an analytical engine that would function using punch cards.
- 1896: Four companies merged and began using the cards for storing data on a larger scale. They originally called themselves the Computing Tabulating Recording Corporation, but later became the International Business Machines Corporation (*that's right* . . . IBM!).

Yadda, yadda, yadda—*badabing*! Modern computers. You're welcome, Bill Gates. His billions are all courtesy of a flimsy card with a bunch of holes punched in it. Who'd have thought?

Now, open the pod bay doors, HAL.

56 SHOPPING CART

TAGLINE: A basket on wheels

PREDECESSOR: A-tisket, a-tasket, a plain ol' basket

LESSON: Make it easier for people to buy stuff and they'll buy more stuff.

Could it be that stores like Sears and J.C. Penney have had slower sales than places like Target and Wal-Mart because of their lack of shopping carts? Now, I don't claim to be exposing a trade secret, *but* it's something to think about as you read how the basket-on-wheels came to be.

The long, strange, squeaky trip started in 1936 when grocery store owner Sylvan Goldman put the first shopping carts into service. Goldman was trying to figure out how to make the shopping experience more efficient so customers would spend more money. So he took a folding chair, put a basket on the seat, wheels on the legs, and—*wham!*—the shopping cart was born. Simple enough, right? Wrong.

It seems shoppers back then didn't take to the carts as well as we do now. Guys thought it was rather sissy to push around a cart while young women found it unfashionable. And old people thought it made them look feeble. (Makes you wonder what they'd think about the motorized scooter version you see today.) But Goldman wasn't about to give up. Like many of the inventions included in this book, marketing played a big part in the shopping cart's popularity.

Goldman hired models to make pushing shopping carts look cool. And it worked. By 1940, shopping carts were so common that supermarkets were redesigned to accommodate them. Nowadays you can't go into a grocery store without seeing them clogging up the aisles, or picking that one with the squeaky, wobbly wheel.

For many, lying down to go to bed meant resting their heads on pieces of wood or slabs of metal.

57 | THE PILLOW

TAGLINE: A soft place to rest your weary head

PREDECESSOR: Harder places to put your head

LESSON: Where heads are concerned, softer is better.

What could be more common than a pillow? Everyone has several, sometimes dozens, even hundreds! (Okay, so not hundreds—but a lot.) You probably can't even imagine trying to sleep without a soft cushion under your head. But that wasn't always the case.

People living in ancient Egypt really lived the hard-knock life. For many, lying down to go to bed meant resting their heads on pieces of wood or slabs of metal. (No wonder they were always at war—they were grumpy from a bad night's sleep.) Back then they believed soft pillows would make it easier for demons to possess their sleeping bodies. So they chose the annoyance of uncomfortable rest over the need for an exorcism.

It took the ingenuity and infamous decadence of the ancient Romans and Greeks to transform the pillow fight into a playful event—as opposed to the bludgeoning bloodbath it was with those Egyptian pillows. These two civilizations went for the softer is better approach, resting their heads on straw and feathers. This idea caught on. Soft pillows and cushions became a sign of prosperity. As the years went by, pillows became fluffier, and those wood and metal Egyptian versions turned into a distant nightmare.

The sale of soft pillows is now a multibillion-dollar industry.

MORE THAN
10,000,000,000
CONDOMS WERE USED
IN 2005.

58 CONDOM

TAGLINE: A super-elastic, ultra-fantastic prophylactic

PREDECESSOR: Disease and unwanted children

LESSON: Sex sells.

Let's take a good long hard look at condoms, shall we? Believe it or not, these things have been around forever.

People who study this sort of thing have found that the use of condoms began around 1000 B.C. However, unlike today's latex or rubber varieties, early condoms were made of linen sheaths, leather, oiled silk paper, or from a very thin hollowed-out horn.

As the story goes, the condom got its name because the popular sheep-entrails variety was first used by farmers in the French town of Condom. While you might find using a sheep's innards as a contraceptive gross, at least it was only intended for a single use. When the less-disgusting rubber condoms came on the scene in 1855, due to their cost, people were advised to wash and reuse them until they fell apart. Now, what's *really* less disgusting? I'd say it's a toss-up.

The latex condom didn't pop up until 1912. The use of latex made the product both affordable and disposable. Goodbye sheep guts and wash-and-wear rubbers. The modern condom was born. But it took until the 1980s and the spread of HIV for people to get over the moral concerns that hampered the invention's acceptance and use. Thankfully, today it's concerning if you *don't* use a condom. And production rates show that people are using them. The United Nations Population Fund reports that over ten billion condoms were used in 2005. And nowadays, you can find them in a variety of colors, textures, and even flavors.

59 | ZIPPER

TAGLINE: Toothy fastening device

PREDECESSOR: Buttons

LESSON: If your design isn't quite where it should be, keep at it or you'll never know.

What's sexier than a woman asking a man (or, hey, another woman) to help zip the back of her dress? Or better yet, to unzip it? Imagine that same romantic moment being interrupted with the loud rip of Velcro. It just wouldn't be the same. While we have several people to thank for the zipper as a mainstay in today's fashion industry, the zipper's rise to prominence wasn't exactly a . . . *zippy* one. It was a rocky start for the humble zipper . . . goulashes were involved . . . I'll explain.

It all began in 1851 when Whitcomb Judson came out with his Clasp Locker device. Judson began marketing his Clasp Locker with businessman Colonel Lewis Walker. The two unveiled their Clasp Locker at the 1893 Chicago World's Fair. It was met with yawns. No one wanted anything to do with Judson and Walker's Locker. In all fairness though, in its original form, it was a pretty scary, medieval-looking thing with big shark-like teeth (seriously).

The two realized something needed to be done. They hired Swedish-born Gideon Sundback, an electrical engineer. He went to work for Judson and Walker's company and redesigned their torturous-looking device into the less-frightening zipper we know today.

However, the name "zipper" was first used by the B. F. Goodrich Company (yeah, those rubber and tire guys). They were using Gideon's fastener on a new type of rubber boot they were calling "galoshes." In addition to Goodrich's galoshes, tobacco pouches were also using the zipper. However, it took twenty more years to convince the fashion industry to seriously promote the zipper on garments.

Today's zippers are used on just about everything. They're common on purses, duffle bags, backpacks, raincoats, jackets, coats, pants, women's dresses, and, of course, leather masks . . . *er* . . . so I've read.

More than 1,000,000,000 Barbies have been sold worldwide.

60 BARBIE DOLL

TAGLINE: Unrealistically skinny adult doll for children

PREDECESSOR: Crappy German doll

LESSON: Girls like to play "dress up."

The doll is believed to be the oldest toy on record. And the Barbie doll is the most popular doll in the history of dolldom. And it's all thanks to Ruth Handler. She invented the busty blonde in 1959, and named it after her daughter Barbara. Her intent was to make the doll a teenage fashion figure.

It all started when Ruth took a trip to Europe and came across the German Bild Lilli doll. It was exactly what she had in mind. She bought three dolls, giving one to Barbara, and brought the other two home to show her husband, an executive at Mattel. She then reworked the design of the German doll and pitched the Barbie doll to Mattel. They loved it. And upon its release, little girls across the United States loved it too. (More than 350,000 Barbies were sold during the first year of production.)

Controversial Figures

If Barbie were a real woman her measurements would be 36-18-38. *Vavoom!* Impressive, but impossible. Her outrageous dimensions caused—and continues to cause—controversy. The fact that the Ken doll has no penis though doesn't seem to bother anyone.

In a move made to solidify Barbie's worldwide domination, Mattel bought the rights to her predecessor, Bild Lilli, in1964. And rather than bring the German doll into Barbie's fold, the company ceased its production. They offed Lilli. With Lilli out of the way, Mattel has gone on to sell more than a billion Barbies worldwide.

Henry Burden further burdened the beast by inventing the horseshoe-manufacturing machine in 1835.

61 HORSESHOE*

TAGLINE: Equine footwear

PREDECESSOR: Barefoot horses

LESSON: Look to a beast to ease your burden.

A horse may be a horse (of course, of course), but a horse without horseshoes is useless. These very simple iron implements play a very significant role in the transportation history of man- and horse-kind.

The idea of the horseshoe goes way back to early Asia, where horsemen fitted what they called "horse booties" on their steeds. Taking it a step further, the ancient Romans slipped trendy sandals made of leather and metal on their horses' hooves. However, the Roman *hipposandals* weren't good enough for European horsemen in the sixth and seventh centuries. (Plus, the horses felt kind of stupid in sandals.) Instead, some horsemen started to nail pieces of metal to the animals' hooves. Things started to take shape during the thirteenth and fourteenth centuries when the widespread manufacturing of iron horseshoes became commonplace.

As for who got lucky when it came to the invention, it wasn't until 1835 that someone really cashed in. That's when Henry Burden created his horseshoe-manufacturing machine, which produced up to sixty shoes an hour. Burden hee-hawed all the way to the bank. And then in 1892, Oscar Brown patented the compound horseshoe that's more along the lines of the shoe used today.

So horses have had a booty, a sandal, and a shoe . . . which means there's still room on the market for a high heel. Get on that!

✳ As in the shoe.

62 HORSESHOES*

TAGLINE: Throwing a horse's shoe at a stick

PREDECESSOR: Just standing around

LESSON: "Almost" counts.

It never ceases to amaze me how sheer boredom can be such a powerful catalyst for invention. It is said that the ancient Greeks developed a sport where the discus was thrown at a stake. But many of the poorer Greeks would play with cast-off horseshoes, which, at the time, were round with a hole in the middle. This game was called *quoits,* and it eventually turned into the game of horseshoes. I'd like to think that the invention of the game of horseshoes went a little something like this . . .

Syphiliticus: I say, Promiscuous, I bet I can throw this sandal of the horse so that it may land upon that stake.

Promiscuous: I think you may be right in your assumption that you can throw that sandal of the horse upon that stake, but we should instead be studying our philosophy and erecting tall marble pillars.

Syphiliticus: While true it may be that we should instead be studying our philosophy and erecting our pillars, throwing this horse's sandal will allow us to procrastinate.

Promiscuous: What role does my cousin Procrastinateus play in this?

Syphiliticus: No Promiscuous, I do not speak of your cousin Procrastinateus. I speak of the *word* procrastinate.

Promiscuous: Ah . . . then we shall make a sport of it and I too shall endeavor to lay that sandal of the horse upon or as close as possible to that stake!

Don't even get me started on Lawn Darts.

✱ As in the game.

WEARING A SEATBELT DIDN'T START TO BECOME MANDATORY UNTIL 1984, WHEN NEW YORK PASSED THE FIRST LAW MAKING IT ILLEGAL TO RIDE IN A CAR WITHOUT WEARING YOUR SEATBELT.

63 SEATBELT

TAGLINE: Helps motorists stop going 70 mph when their cars do

PREDECESSOR: An untimely introduction to your windshield

LESSON: Use your head to make an impression on something other than the dashboard.

Seatbelts are one heck of a lifesaver, aren't they? So logical and simple you'd think they would've come standard with the wheel (page 39). But, no. *Why?* Because no one capitalized on the opportunity. In fact, it took until the 1950s for seatbelts to start showing up in cars. That's over *fifty* years after the first automobile was invented in 1870.

Even after manufacturers were required to install seatbelts in the 1960s, people didn't use them. I remember back when I was a kid in the '70s and '80s, my parents would drive along the interstate at 75 miles per hour while my friends and I crawled around freely in the back seat, unbelted, smoking cigars, drinking beer, and gambling on dog races. Man, those were the days.

The invention of the over-the-lap seatbelt is attributed to English engineer George Cayley; he came up with the concept in the late 1800s. However, the patent for the first automobile seatbelt belongs to Edward J. Claghorn. His patent was issued in 1885. And it showed up first in American models by Nash and Ford, but only as optional add-ons. Saab was the first to place them in cars as standard equipment in 1958.

It took a few years for seatbelts to become standard in automobiles, and it took even longer for them to be used regularly. Wearing a seatbelt didn't start to become mandatory until 1984, when New York passed the first law making it illegal to ride in a car without wearing your seatbelt. Since then, seatbelts have saved millions of lives, are standard in every car, and their use is mandatory nearly everywhere.

64 SPEAR

TAGLINE: A pointy stick

PREDECESSOR: A stick with less poking ability

LESSON: Monkeys are like really hairy people.

Here's an invention so simple that even monkeys use it. Think hunting and warfare are just human pastimes? Think again.

The common chimpanzee has been known to manufacture and use the spear. Chimpanzees near Kédougou, Senegal, have been seen fashioning spears by breaking limbs from trees, sharpening one end with their teeth, and then, apparently, using the weapons to hunt galagos, a lemur like primate. Orangutans have also been witnessed using spears. Rather than hunt other primates though, they use the tool to fish, having observed humans fishing in similar ways. Smart little devils.

It's been suggested that the discovery of the primates' use of spears means early humans used spears as well, perhaps even as early as five million years ago. And they have been used for hunting, defense, and warfare ever since.

It's just a pointy stick, but somebody had to think of it. And if a monkey can invent stuff, cheer up, so can you!

Spears with a Pointed Past

- Gáe Bulga: Weapon wielded by Cúchulainn, a hero in ancient Celtic mythology
- Gungnir: The spear belonging to the Norse god Odin
- The Spear of Destiny: Used to pierce Jesus' side while he was crucified
- Spear of Fuchai: Ancient weapon of the King of Fuchai
- Trishula: Three-pronged spear held by the Hindu god Shiva

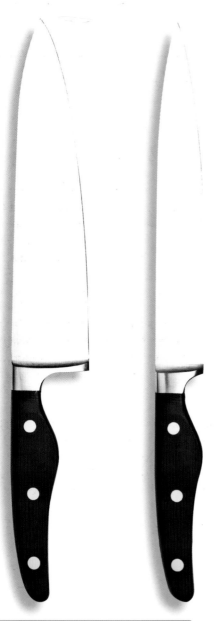

KNIVES STARTED
OUT BEING MADE
FROM CHIPPED
VOLCANIC ROCK
AS FAR BACK
AS 2.6 MILLION
YEARS AGO.

65 KNIFE

TAGLINE: Sharp object that cuts, stabs, and butters

PREDECESSOR: Ripping stuff

LESSON: You have to be sharp to invent sharp things.

The knife! It slices! It dices! It can cut through a tin can and still *make a clean cut through a tomato!* But wait! *There's more . . .*

Knives have always been valuable tools. They started out being made from chipped volcanic rock as far back as 2.6 *million* years ago, with artifacts being found in the Afar region of Ethiopia. Similar tools were made throughout the Paleolithic era from animal bone and wood. And up until relatively recently—about ten thousand years ago—these were the main materials used to make knives.

Incredible, but true! Still not convinced that the knife is one of the most useful tools ever invented? Wait 'til you hear this!

The knife improved with advances in metallurgy (that's a hell of a word, isn't it? It's the study of metallic elements). Knives made of bone and wood became a thing of the past. Now it was all about the cutting power of steel. Cold, hard steel. And ever since then they've been the go-to item no matter what the need—whether it's eviscerating your mortal enemy or buttering your toast.

They slice! They dice! They stab! They poke! They slather! Knives! Now how much would you pay? Wait! Don't answer that! There's still more!

Today we slice, dice, and schmere with: bread knives, dive knives, hunting knives, stockman knives, scalpels, utility knives, cooking knives, filet knives, Bowie knives, pocket knives, switch blades, electric knives . . . the list goes on!

Available at a certified dealer near you! Act now!

DID YOU KNOW?

The Japanese have cultivated square watermelons to save space and so they stack and transport more easily.

66 | FARMING

TAGLINE: Growing stuff

PREDECESSOR: Foraging for stuff

LESSON: Get your hands dirty.

The first time I planted a tomato I was absolutely astonished that the thing actually grew, and beyond that, it produced fruit that I could consume! It was a powerful feeling. So much so that it makes me wonder why it took so damn long for mankind to get the picture and start farming. Yet it did.

The roots of farming (pun definitely intended) are in the present-day Middle East and Turkey, and were laid about ten thousand years ago. That's right. Not one hundred thousand or one million years ago—ten thousand. Nothing against prehistoric man, but why didn't someone in the hunter/gatherer society decide to be a cultivator sooner? It wouldn't have been a question of technology. All they needed was right there: seeds, dirt, water, sun. But alas, it was an opportunity lost. Instead, the inventor honor was bestowed on the Catal Hüyük and Jericho farming settlements. And what an honor that is, as the concept quite literally feeds the world to this day.

Catal Hüyük and Jericho started the agricultural process around 7000 B.C. Evidence has been found of the people using grasses for food and planting seeds for harvest. These early crops have been identified as cereals—the same foodstuffs that make up the majority of the world's modern food supply.

There are over 2.1 million farms in the United Sates alone. With a cluck-cluck here and a moo-moo there, old McDonald and his pals farm over 900 million acres. Worldwide, food is harvested from an estimated 37.7 percent of the planet's land surfaces.

Franklin's Funnier Fodder

Some of his more humorous (and coherent) quotations include:

- "Three may keep a secret, if two of them are dead."
- "Certainty? In this world nothing is certain but death and taxes."
- "God heals and the doctor takes the fee."
- "Guests, like fish, begin to smell after three days."
- "If you would know the value of money try to borrow some."
- "Keep your eyes wide open before marriage, and half-shut afterwards."

67 LIGHTNING ROD

TAGLINE: A metal stick

PREDECESSOR: Buildings being destroyed by lightning

LESSON: Ben Franklin is *the man*.

We all have our favorite American founding father. Mine is Ben Franklin. He did it all. He was a publisher, inventor, scientist, politician, writer, and philosopher. And, man, was that guy funny!

Although most of his inventions are ingenious and complicated—and therefore not included in this book—there is one that is simplistically brilliant: The lightning rod. Of course, at the time, inventing the lightning rod was pure genius, and his experiments with electricity were unprecedented and led to a unique understanding of lightning. But come on. It was a piece of metal. Of course lightning would strike it. However, without his groundbreaking lightning experimentation and vast knowledge of the subject, we may be without this simple yet extraordinarily effective device.

Once Franklin understood that lightning is an electrical force, he thought of a very simple way to protect tall buildings from lightning strikes. All you have to do is attach a grounded metal rod to the top of each building. The lightning would be attracted to the rod instead of the structure, thereby preventing damage and fires.

Today, literally every tall structure has a Franklin lightning rod. Many of us are alive to create, invent, and discover because of it. Simple yet brilliant. It embodies the very spirit of this book, and should be an inspiration to us all.

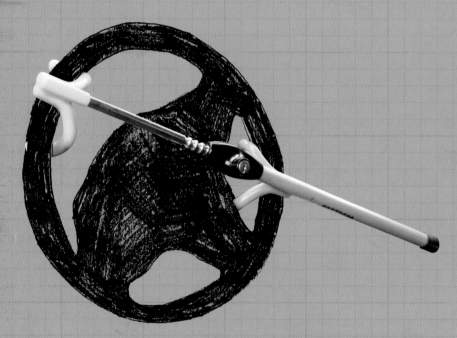

THE CLUB REMAINS ONE OF
THE MOST EFFECTIVE WAYS
TO PREVENT CAR THEFT.

68 THE CLUB

TAGLINE: A metal protector

PREDECESSOR: More stolen cars

LESSON: Keep it simple. Keep it safe.

It's the middle of the night. You're sleeping peacefully, dreaming of things you can invent to make millions of dollars, and you're just about to have your Aha! moment when . . . *beep, beep, beep, whee-ooo, whee-ooo, beep, beep, beep* . . . somebody's freakin' car alarm ruins your inspirational slumber! Do you rush to the window to see if it's being stolen? Do you call the police? Do you try and thwart the thieves? *No!* Because 9.8 times out of 10, it's a false alarm! And even if it weren't, studies have shown that the car alarm doesn't even prevent a thief from stealing an automobile. What's really needed is something simple, obvious, and *silent*. Just the kind of thing you might find in this book, something like . . . The Club!

Winner International's popular automotive steering wheel lock is the perfect deterrent, whether you hope to keep your car safe or get a good night's sleep. For those not familiar with the device, it consists of two metal pieces fastened together to form one long bar that when extended and locked makes the wheel impossible to turn.

It's believed that its inventor, James E. Winner Jr., came up with the idea during his service in the Korean War. There, he was instructed to secure the steering wheels of Jeeps with metal chains. Like the Jeep chains, The Club limits the movement of the steering wheel and is difficult to remove without the help of a hacksaw. And sawing takes time—a precious commodity for car thieves.

The Club remains one of the most effective ways to prevent car theft. Millions of units are sold each year. So, do us all a favor: Buy The Club and turn off your stupid car alarm so we can all get some sleep!

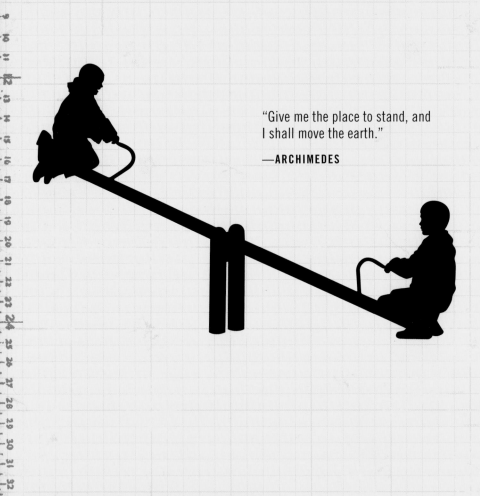

"Give me the place to stand, and I shall move the earth."

—ARCHIMEDES

69 LEVER

TAGLINE: A prying and lifting device

PREDECESSOR: Hernias

LESSON: Sometimes inventions are so simple they just occur naturally, so keep your eyes peeled.

What do you say when someone has an advantage over a particular situation? Well, you might just say they have *leverage*. Why? Because the word's derived from *lever*, which provides an enormous advantage in power over anything upon which it is used.

Follow? Good. Let's think about the lever's use by taking a stroll down memory lane to a more innocent time when you spent your younger days on the playground. You see another kid sitting on one end of the seesaw. You run over to the opposite side, looking to climb on. That other kid is kinda big though. You're worried you won't be able to move her an inch off the ground. But miraculously when you climb on, she rises into the sky and then she comes back down and you rise up. *The power of the lever!* And then she jumps off while you're still lifted and you crash to the ground for the tenth time today even though she promised she wouldn't do it again so you spend the next twenty-five years of your life harboring mistrust issues and resentment and . . . *ahem* . . . sorry. Back to *the power of the lever!*

The seesaw is a simple example of how this simple machine works. The lever is one of the most useful basic tools. While the lever itself isn't an actual "invention," the concept has been utilized in a number of important ones. It's helped do everything. The ancient Egyptians used levers to raise tremendous stones, sometimes weighing more than 200 tons. As for a modern use—just think of how much more weight you can move in a wheelbarrow. Why? Because of the *lever*!

And many other basic tools we use everyday are levers, including scissors, pliers, hammer claws, nutcrackers, and tongs. But my favorite use will always be the seesaw! (Oh and I'll get you Judy Warkaminsky—it may have been in the fourth grade, but I remember . . . oh I remember . . . .)

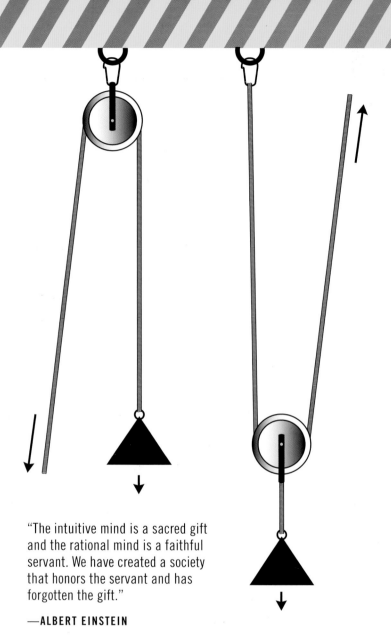

"The intuitive mind is a sacred gift and the rational mind is a faithful servant. We have created a society that honors the servant and has forgotten the gift."

—ALBERT EINSTEIN

70 | PULLEY

TAGLINE: Ingenious yanking device

PREDECESSOR: Grunting more

LESSON: Help people move things and you'll be remembered.

Ever lowered a Venetian blind? You've used a pulley. Ever raised a flag? Pulled up an anchor? Well then, you've used a pulley. Get the pulley picture? Like the lever, the pulley makes it a whole lot easier to lift things. In fact, the two use some of the same principles.

There are many uses for this device, but one of the most important was its nautical application. As people started to transport goods over longer distances by sea they used the pulley to hoist the ship's sails just as you might use it to lift your Venetian blinds. Without the use of this modest device, early sea travel would have been thwarted, goods and ideas would not have traveled as easily to different lands, and culture and civilization, as we know it, might not be quite the same.

Let's assume that's a good thing.

Get the idea? Pulley power is a plus.

The Simple Machines
A simple machine is a basic device that magnifies force. There are six simple machines that are the basis of all machines. They are:

- Inclined plane
- Lever
- Pulley
- Screw
- Wedge
- Wheel and axle

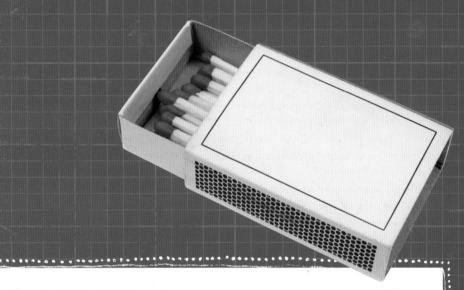

Taft's Tax Trick

The reliable ignition of a fire was deemed so important that President William H. Taft persuaded Diamond Match to release its patent for "the good of mankind." Diamond Match complied. And on January 28, 1911, Congress promptly placed a high tax on matches.

D-oh!

71 MATCHES

TAGLINE: Sticks that light on fire

PREDECESSOR: Lighting sticks on fire

LESSON: Make the ignition of controlled fire easier and it will sell.

Here's another example of it taking *for-ev-er* to put two seemingly obvious things together to come up with a good idea.

Fire is one of the most basic and essential human needs. But before the match, starting a fire was not that simple. Even though one of the main components of the match—phosphorous—was discovered in 1669, it took until 1827 for the first practical match to be invented. It came about when John Walker, an English chemist and apothecary, coated the end of a stick with the material and realized he could quickly light the stick on fire by striking it against a rough surface. Convenient, but toxic—Walker's match let off poisonous fumes.

Two more inventors followed in Walker's footsteps. Samuel Jones came up with his own version he called "Lucifers." Unfortunately, these little devils also let off harmful smoke. And then Swede Johan Edvard Lundstrom patented his own version of the fire-starters in 1855. He even separated the phosphorus from the other ingredients by putting it on a sandpaper strip affixed to the outside of the box and the rest of the materials in the match head. Still not safe smoke though. (It'd kill you if you breathed enough of it.)

Finally, in 1910, a nonpoisonous match was made. Using a chemical called sesquisulfide of phosphorous, the Diamond Match Company managed to achieve what was out of the other three's reach—the nontoxic match. This formula is still used in the modern match you light up today.

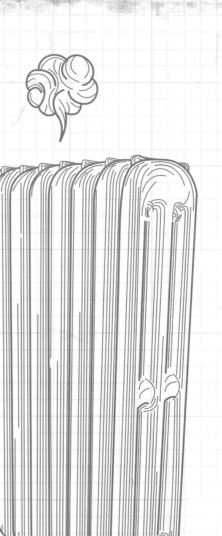

72 RADIANT HEAT IN HOMES

TAGLINE: Hot water percolator for your house

PREDECESSOR: Open flames which were less efficient and more deadly

LESSON: Create items that address basic human needs.

Humans need to be warm. That's why fire (page 81) was such a big hit. Before radiators people heated their homes and buildings using fire in fireplaces or stoves. In fact Benjamin Franklin's "Franklin Stove" was his most popular invention and the primary means of heating dwellings before radiant heat. Problem was, you had to frequently refuel, and they would occasionally cause a fire, which would burn all your worldly possessions and kill your family. Radiant heat is cheaper and safer because it uses water.

Here's how it works: It's kind of like one of those old percolator coffee pots, or one of those steamers used to get the wrinkles out of your clothes. A boiler heats water, which flows or is pumped through pipes to each radiation device. The radiators transfer heat from the water to the air, warming your home. So, basically, it's boiling water with some simple plumbing involved.

An American, William Baldwin, invented the radiator. By the start of the twentieth century his cast iron radiator system brought central heating into the homes of most Americans. It made him a very rich man and it made a lot of people a lot safer.

73 FINGERPRINT DETECTION

TAGLINE: The original *CSI*

PREDECESSOR: A funny hat, magnifying glass, and Dr. Watson

LESSON: Crime doesn't pay; solving crime does.

People had been around for thousands of years before somebody looked down at her hand and noticed that we all have different fingerprints. Today we consider Henry Faulds, a Scottish scientist who published an article on the subject in 1880, to be the "Father of Fingerprinting" even though he never received any real recognition for it during his day.

A few years after Faulds, Sir Edward Henry and Sir Francis Galton became interested in the technique. (Galton was Charles Darwin's cousin by the way.) Both of these men helped to create a system for "lifting" and tracking fingerprints, but for rather different reasons. Henry was the one interested in using fingerprinting to identify criminals. Whereas, Galton was more interested in using fingerprints to determine desirable characteristics in people (kind of like examining the lumps on a person's head or Phrenology, which was also a popular practice during the nineteenth century). He hoped to use the technology to find the key to the "Master Race." That's probably why modern fingerprinting is referred to as the "Henry Method" and not the "Crazy Racist Galton Method."

The FBI currently has a database of over 60 million fingerprints. Although it is beginning to be eclipsed by advances in DNA research, fingerprint files remain the most common tool for identifying people.

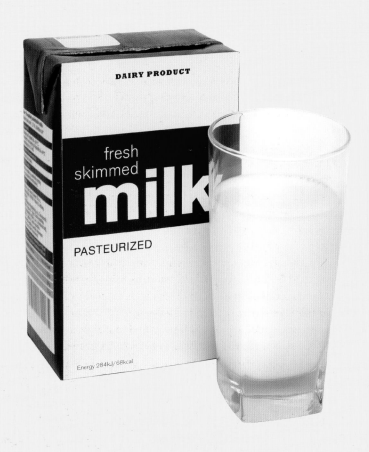

DAIRY PRODUCT

fresh
skimmed
milk

PASTEURIZED

Energy 284kJ/68kcal

74 PASTEURIZATION

TAGLINE: Boiling stuff to kill varmints and germs before they enter your bloodstream

PREDECESSOR: Salmonella

LESSON: Make people healthier.

It's easy to point fingers at our predecessors in amazement, and wonder why it took them so long to figure out the seemingly obvious. And I certainly do my fair share of just that in this book. But it has always amazed me that it took us so long to conceive of the causes of infection and the existence of germs. Sure, people couldn't *see* germs and bacteria back then, but there were lots of things they believed in that they couldn't see. (Read: religion.)

Sadly, three of Louis Pasteur's five children died from typhoid fever before he looked into the deadly germs that were being bottled up with milk. In his early years, Pasteur was a researcher for wine growers in France, and helped them with perfecting the fermentation process. There, he began to develop ways to kill or "pasteurize" germs.

Unlike sterilization, pasteurization is not meant to destroy all microorganisms in the food or liquid in question, such as milk. Instead, pasteurization reduces the amount of viable pathogens so they are unlikely to cause disease. To do this, Pasteur simply perfected a way of heating milk to a set temperature for a set period of time. This method is still used today in various forms, but remains essentially the same as it was in Pasteur's day.

DID YOU KNOW?

Henry Ford only offered his Model T in black because that was the fastest drying paint he could find.

75 | ASSEMBLY LINE

TAGLINE: Division of labor in order to increase manufacturing speed

PREDECESSOR: Individual craftsmen

LESSON: Grouping like tasks makes anything go faster. (Just ask Lucy and Ethel.*)

Like many simple ideas, the assembly line was not "invented" per se at one time by one person. It has been independently developed and redeveloped throughout history based on logic. However, its explosive influence in the late nineteenth century and beginning of the twentieth can be attributed to two men—Ransom E. Olds and Henry Ford—who profited greatly from this concept.

> "A business that makes nothing but money is a poor business."
>
> —HENRY FORD

Prior to the twentieth century, manufactured products were crafted individually by hand. Individual craftsmen would use their knowledge, which was often developed through extensive apprenticeships, to make something from nothing. Some, in fact *most* people, believe that this produced a higher quality product. However, sometimes quantity is needed over quality.

Many think that it was Henry Ford who invented the assembly line. This is incorrect. What Ford did do was improve upon the concept created by Ransom E. Olds—founder of Oldsmobile—by implementing conveyor belts. This cut the time of manufacturing a Model T Ford from a day and a half to ninety minutes.

✳ Oh, Lucy. I love you, but when will you learn?

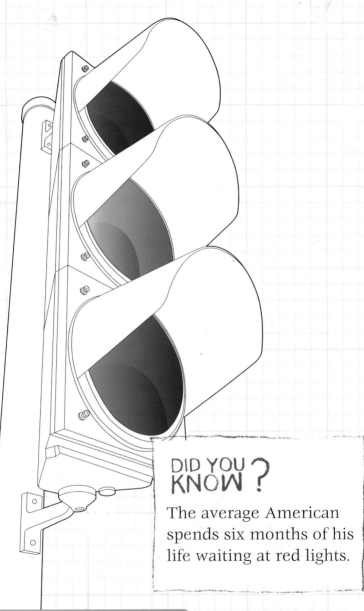

DID YOU KNOW ?

The average American
spends six months of his
life waiting at red lights.

76 TRAFFIC LIGHT

TAGLINE: Traffic's guiding light

PREDECESSOR: A policeman at every intersection

LESSON: Police should be catching bad guys, not standing around in intersections.

Before the traffic light, a police officer would be stationed full time at intersections to direct traffic—a practice still utilized today, though only in worst-case scenarios. The first attempt to reduce the number of police needed to direct traffic at intersections was before the automobile, when traffic consisted of pedestrians, buggies, and wagons.

The first traffic light lit up in 1868 and was a revolving lantern that used red and green signals to control traffic at a London intersection. Yet, it still required a police officer. He had to turn the lantern so that the appropriate signal faced the right lane of traffic. Not only is this incredibly stupid, as the officer essentially was doing the same thing he was before, but the device also had the misfortune of exploding into a fiery blaze one afternoon, injuring the policeman who was operating it and several passersby. Back to the drawing board.

> "I have not failed. I've just found 10,000 ways that won't work."
>
> **—THOMAS A. EDISON**

In 1923, American Garrett Morgan was busy developing a device that could help control traffic in Cleveland, Ohio. Rather than use a lantern and policeman like the London version, Morgan decided electric and automatic was the way to go. His patent for the first successful traffic light was bought by General Electric. The company took the patent and ran, building a monopoly on traffic-light manufacturing, and gave us the red-yellow-green light we know today.

Red for stop. Green for go. And yellow for speed up.

"Owing to this struggle for life, any variation, however slight and from whatever cause proceeding, if it be in any degree profitable to an individual of any species, in its infinitely complex relationship to other organic beings and to external nature, will tend to the preservation of that individual, and will generally be inherited by its offspring."

—CHARLES DARWIN,
ON THE ORIGIN OF SPECIES

77 | THE THEORY OF EVOLUTION

TAGLINE: Only the strong survive

PREDECESSOR: God

LESSON: Sometimes the greatest ideas in the world are right before our eyes the whole time.

Everybody's all, "*Oh!* The theory of evolution! How groundbreaking and smart!" Um . . . have you ever looked at a monkey and noticed how much they look like us? It's just that simple really.

Not to say that I could've thought it up. But come on. This "elegant" theory is a perfect example of how such an amazingly obvious idea can go unnoticed for centuries until one person comes along and gets famous from it.

But did you know that Charles Darwin wasn't the first person to bring it up?

Revolutionary evolutionary ideas have been around since the sixth century B.C. Way back then, Greek philosopher Anaximander was examining and expanding on theories of evolution. And he wasn't the only one. Greek philosophers Empedocles and Lucretius, Arab biologist Al-Jahiz, and Persian philosopher Ibn Miskawayh all threw their hats into the evolutionary ring. And the list doesn't even end there (though for the purposes of this book, it does) and it doesn't even begin to include all the indigenous people of various lands who have woven this theory into their cultural and religious belief systems for thousands of years undocumented.

However as far as western civilization is concerned, it was Charles Darwin who popularized the idea that we evolved from apes. His *On the Origin of Species* brought the idea of natural selection into the collective conversation. The 1859 publication still stands as the bible of evolutionary theory to this day.

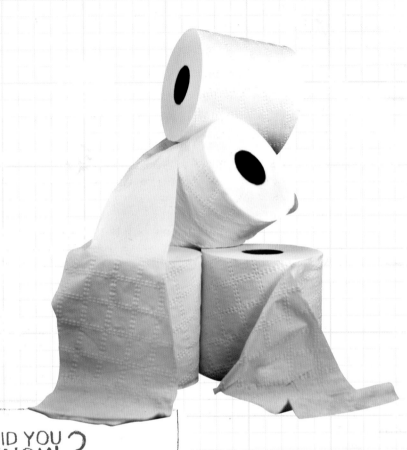

DID YOU KNOW ?

Each year, there are more than 40,000 toilet related injuries in the United States alone.

78 TOILET PAPER

TAGLINE: Paper with which one wipes his or her ass

PREDECESSOR: See first paragraph below

LESSON: Make it more convenient and, yes, pleasant, for people to do the things that everybody does and nobody talks about.

Wool, lace, hemp, hay, rags, grass, leaves, snow, fruit peels, the pages in this book, seashells, clams, moss, corn cobs, wood shavings, seaweed, corn husks, animal furs, sticks, feathers, a baby chicken, dead rats, *etcetera*—all early substitutes for TP.

And when those weren't used, one's bare hand was always a possible solution. In fact, it was common practice all over the world, from Europe to South America to India, to use the left hand for wiping and the right hand for greeting.

However, the Romans and Chinese weren't really down with the left-hand wipe. Instead, the Romans used a sponge on a stick to clean after doing their business. And when they were done, the sponge went into a bucket of water to "clean" it for the next person. It took the Chinese, who invented actual paper, to provide a paper-alternative to all the other cleaning products.

Modern toilet paper wasn't manufactured until 1907, when the Scott Paper Company rolled it out. The fact that the company's still around today proves how well the public (and their asses) took to the product.

79 SHOELACE

TAGLINE: A string with which to tie your shoe

PREDECESSOR: A buckle

LESSON: Make good things better.

The first "shoes" were a simple hide or covering bound to the foot with either leather thongs, grasses, or some form of twine and fashioned by the prehistoric tribe known as the Reebokians.* The recent discovery of the bronze-age Ötzi or the Iceman, who is thought to have lived around 3000 B.C., revealed fairly complex insulated leather kicks bound with "shoelaces." Not exactly Nikes, but still it's pretty impressive.

The shoelace is one of those inventions/discoveries that everyone simply takes for granted. But they really weren't widely used until the 1800s. Before that, shoes were fastened with buckles or even buttons. Most experts believe that the adaptation of the shoelace was a technical advancement. I disagree. I think that the shoelace became widely used when it was discovered that pointing at someone's feet and saying, "Your shoe's unbuckled . . . *gotcha!*" didn't get the same amount of laughs as the shoelace gag.

> "Truth is ever to be found in simplicity, and not in the multiplicity and confusion of things."
>
> **—ISAAC NEWTON**

The first person to capitalize on the shoelace was Harvey Kennedy. He apparently made $2.5 million after patenting the shoelace in 1790. But did he actually *invent* the shoelace, or just take advantage of a commonly practiced idea? As I've stated before, *it doesn't matter*—the guy made a ton of money.

* Yeah, you got me.

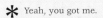

BOSTON

LONDON

SYDNEY

DID YOU KNOW ?

A "jiffy" is an actual unit. It was invented in the early 1900s by Gilbert Newton Lewis. In fact, the jiffy is exactly 1/100th of a second. Though it also has different measurements depending upon the field of study to which it is applied.

80 STANDARDIZED TIME

TAGLINE: Time so everybody knows what time it is at the same time

PREDECESSOR: I'll tell you in exactly one minute

LESSON: Use your head and your watch.

No one really knows what time standard time was implemented in the United States. However, we do know the country's railroads started using standard time zones on November 18, 1883. The ingenious plan in place before that? Locality and winging it.

See, before time became standardized, it was approximate, by locality, believe it or not. Each region maintained its own time by means of a local, well-known clock. For example, sometimes it was a public clock maintained by the town (think Big Ben). Sometimes it was simply set by the clocks in an established clock or jewelry store window.

Sure, it was roughly the same, and new technologies such as the telegraph helped matters, but time zones were difficult to account for, and often ignored completely.

As populations grew, and technology advanced, the use of standard time gradually became more common and necessary—which, in turn made communication and travel more efficient. Standard time in time zones took a bit longer to come around. In fact, the practice of establishing different time zones in the United States was not mandated by Federal law until March 19, 1918, with the legislation called the Standard Time Act. Catchy!

DID YOU KNOW ?

President Eisenhower implemented the concept of the interstate highway system, and the federal law mandating that one in every five miles of federal highway be straight. This is so the straight sections can be used as airstrips during times of war or other national emergencies.

81 ROAD SIGNS

TAGLINE: Directional indications on travel routes

PREDECESSOR: Asking if you can get there from here

LESSON: People generally like to know where the hell they are.

The first road sign was a Roman milestone. No, I don't think you understand. They were literally Roman *mile*stones, indicating the distance and direction to Rome. Thus the meaning of the word "milestone" and the saying, "All roads lead to Rome." In the Middle Ages, these milestones evolved into multidirectional signs. Sure, sometimes they were adorned with the heads of that particular township's enemies, but nevertheless they were helpful, as established intersections became more common.

In 1895, an Italian Touring Club created what's believed to be the first modern road sign system. Europe's then International League of Touring Organizations advocated for such a system to be adopted throughout the continent. However, it was never approved because it was thought to be a bit *too* helpful and much less entertaining for the locals—who spent most of their days amusing themselves by watching Americans and Canadians wander about hopelessly lost.

These days, traffic signs are everywhere. In fact, we now have just the opposite problem: too many signs! Now we are witnessing the advent of the more commonly seen, new generation of "intelligent" signs. This signage can actually adjust its messages and signals to adapt to road conditions and traffic flow as needed.

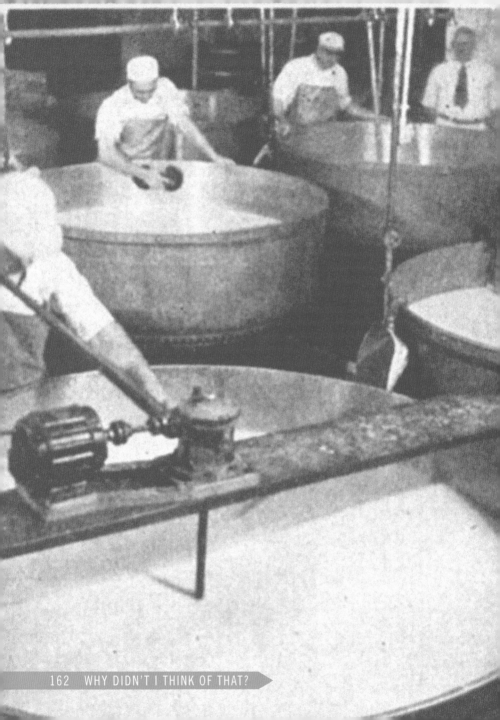

82 MASS PRODUCTION

TAGLINE: Producing a whole mess of stuff

PREDECESSOR: Producing one thing at a time

LESSON: Seek efficiency.

This is really more of a philosophy than an invention per se, but I have included it here because there were a few individuals who recognized its enormous potential and capitalized upon it. The concept is simple. (Starting to recognize a theme in this book?)

Let's say that you're making a widget. The more efficiently you crank out your widgets, the faster you can make them. The faster you make them, the more money you make. The more money you make, the lower the price to the consumer . . . next thing you know, you've cornered the market and are the king of widgets. Congratulations.

The Henry Ford Motor Company popularized mass production in the early twentieth century. They achieved this by introducing electric motors to the then-well-known technique of chain or sequential production. This began a new era often called the "second industrial revolution." And making the Model T affordable to most consumers.

The preceding American system of manufacturing relied on steam power. This new technology in mass production factories was electric, and used sophisticated, pointy, razor-sharp, bone-crushing machinery. Adoption of these techniques coincided with the beginning of the second industrial revolution and the United States' emergence as the dominant industrial superpower of the twentieth century. It also coincided with the advent of Unions and Worker's rights. Because in our haste to make more for less, many of the factory line workers employed to make widgets lost their digits.

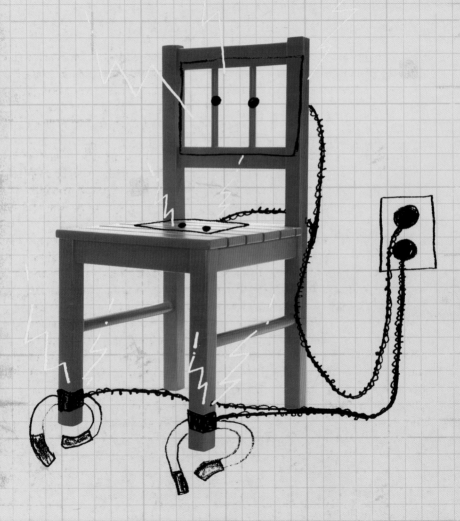

83 ELECTRIC CHAIR

TAGLINE: A very uncomfortable seat

PREDECESSOR: Chairs that didn't kill you

LESSON: Look for efficient "painless" ways to kill one another.

Unpleasant as this may be, it's a very simple and good idea. As is the case with the guillotine (page 13), people have been trying to find simple, efficient ways to execute one another for thousands of years. And it's not as easy as it seems. For example: Take this scene from a Texas jailhouse on June 24, 1987—in an effort to administer a lethal injection to Elliott Johnson, it took thirty-five minutes to insert a needle into his vein.

Hanging (the most popular form of execution) was no picnic either. A good deal of experimentation had to be done to determine the proper drop-to-weight ratio. Too short a drop, the neck isn't snapped and the victim dies a horribly slow strangulation. Too long a drop and the victim's head pops off like a cork.

So, Harold Brown had the idea that electricity would be the new and improved, humane way to get the job done. To prove the efficiency of his electric chair in order to secure a patent, Brown started demonstrating the machine's killing ability by using it on cats and dogs. Even with his trial runs on Fluffy and Rover, the New York Commission still wasn't sold on the idea. So Brown fried himself up some steak. He brought a cow before the panel of patent officials and flipped the switch. But Brown's animal kingdom killing spree didn't stop there. He also offed a horse, an elephant, and an orangutan—which ended up catching on fire. (Man, he's lucky PETA wasn't around back then.) Finally the commission was convinced of the invention's efficiency and the electric chair became an official means of execution on June 4, 1888.

DID YOU KNOW ?

Battery manufacturer and innovator, Duracell, built portions of its new international headquarters using its own waste materials.

REDUCE
REUSE
RECYCLE

84 RECYCLING

TAGLINE: Global hand-me-downs

PREDECESSOR: Making that poor Native American from the commercial cry

LESSON: "Save the Planet" my ass! The planet will be just fine without humans.

Think your fancy recycling bins are something new? Nope. Just ask your grandparents who suffered through WWII. They were recycling back then just to get America through the war. Citizens were encouraged to plant "victory gardens" to conserve food. There were "metal drives" to help with the conservation of iron, tin, and copper. In fact, the 1942 U.S. penny was minted in zinc so that more copper would be available for the war effort. So don't think you're so special.

Recycling has been a matter of environmental or economic concern in one form or another since the dawn of man. The only thing that's really changed is that the advent of the industrial age has finally screwed up the environment enough for us to notice. The good news is, we are finally taking action. Recycling has become a huge and profitable industry, creating more opportunities for small and large companies. But, the conservation of our elements and necessities in order to sustain our lives as human beings has been a consistent element of our fundamental survival.

Today, city officials can sub-contract with privately owned companies, creating new opportunities in the private sector and making recycling one of the fastest growing industries on the planet.

DID YOU KNOW?

The first Coca-Cola bottling facility was built in Chattanooga, Tennessee.

85 · BOTTLING

TAGLINE: Putting stuff in bottles

PREDECESSOR: Putting stuff in glasses

LESSON: Think up cool and refreshing ideas.

Bottling, in many forms, has been around for quite some time; it's been used for wine and other liquors for centuries. But, believe it or not, no one really thought to use it for nonalcoholic purposes until 1894. And it all began with Coca-Cola. They taught the world to bottle in *per-fect har-mo-ny*.

However, it wasn't the company that began the bottling phenomenon. It was shopkeeper Joseph A. Biedenham. The Mississippi candy-store owner thought to capitalize on the success of the new fountain drink by putting it into bottles so that his customers could take it on the go.

Bottling on a more massive scale didn't come about until two lawyers, Benjamin F. Thomas and Joseph B. Whitehead, saw what a goldmine bottling soft drinks could be. The two approached the Coca-Cola Company with their idea, and with some serious coaxing the two attorneys-turned-entrepreneurs were able to convince the company president to sign over the bottling rights. The first bottling plant was established in 1899 and within ten years 400 Coca-Cola bottling plants were in full operation. Noting the success of the venture between Coca-Cola and the bottlers, other beverage manufacturers began to follow suit and started bottling their soft drinks.

So the next time you crack open your favorite beverage, ask yourself, "Why didn't I think of something like this?"

> "He who pours water hastily into a bottle spills more than goes in."
>
> **—SPANISH PROVERB**

86 THE WINDSHIELD

TAGLINE: Shields against the wind

PREDECESSOR: Goggles

LESSON: If you have to pick bugs out of your teeth, there is probably a potential product there.

What came before the windshield? Well, in the beginning, motorists were protected by two glass plates that were about three inches in diameter, fitting over each of the driver's eyes. That's right. Before the windshield, drivers wore goggles.

Like most features in the auto industry, the windshield started as a luxury add-on and not a standard feature. It makes you wonder what exactly came standard on a car back then.

The first windshields were originally made of plate glass. So, if an accident occurred, it was fairly certain that you would become shredded like a hunk of Parmesan cheese. But safety was a concern back then . . . sort of. Since the wiper hadn't been invented yet, the windshield was made up of two pieces connected by a horizontal hinge. So if the windshield became too dirty, the driver could fold it down. Hope they kept those goggles handy.

Despite their necessity, the windshield's tendency to kill and maim drivers made it a rather risky feature. Luckily though, safety glass soon followed. Developed by Edouard Benedictu and John C. Wood, the plate glass alternative is still used in today's windshields.

87 | WINDSHIELD WIPER

TAGLINE: Device that allows you to drive in the rain without dying

PREDECESSOR: Squinting and cursing and crashing

LESSON: Protect your patents.

While the automobile isn't included in this book (because it's a rather complicated device), just about every accessory we take for granted today has found a home in these pages, including this entry—the original windshield wiper, which would be paired with the windshield (page 171) and replaced by the intermittent windshield wiper (page 175).

In addition to being a lesson on accessorizing, the windshield wiper also teaches novice inventors to check expirations dates closely (and not just on that milk that's been in the fridge for a couple of weeks). As it turns out, the original wiper patent was allowed to expire. Mary Anderson, of New York City, was granted the patent in 1903. Her original pitch to companies to begin producing the device didn't work out. But rather than keep at it, Mary put the patent in a drawer and gave up. A big mistake for Mary and any other would-be inventor out there with a dream. Rule number one: If you believe, *never give up*.

This allowed Fred and William Folberth to swoop in and steal Mary's squeegying thunder. The two came up with their spin on the automatic windshield wiper in 1921 and called it the Folberths. The device quickly went from optional to standard and the Folberths started raking in the dough.

So, keep your eyes peeled for ways to build on an already existing idea, because often one great idea would not be possible without another. For example, the windshield wiper would be rather excessive without the previous entry in this book.

Inventions in the Movies
This complicated story is depicted in the 2008 movie *Flash of Genius* starring Greg Kinnear.

88 INTERMITTENT WINDSHIELD WIPER

TAGLINE: A —wi — per — that — wipes—in — ter — mit — tent — ly

PREDECESSOR: A wiper that just wipes

LESSON: There are people who *will* steal your ideas. Be careful.

Looking for something to do on a rainy day? How 'bout making $29 million, but waiting thirty-eight years to collect it?

The inventor of intermittent windshield wipers, Robert Kearns did just that. He was awarded a multimillion-dollar settlement after suing Ford and Chrysler, granted it was almost *four decades* after he invented them. Kearns held a number of patents for his windshield-wiper design that let drivers choose the speed at which their wipers swept the windshield clean.

Shortly after offering his invention to various automakers to no avail, several of them began to mysteriously include intermittent windshield wipers on their vehicles. Keams was all "*What the hell?!*" and promptly sued Ford Motor Company and Chrysler for patent infringement.

This all happened in the late '70s and early '80s, but this poor bastard had to wait until the '90s for a jury to finally decide that Ford did indeed infringe on his patent. Complicated court hearing after court hearing ensued, and Ford ultimately agreed to pay $10.2 million. Kearns was also awarded $18.7 million from Chrysler. But, believe it or not, Kearns' later lawsuit against General Motors and foreign carmakers was dismissed.

Watch your backs, inventors.

Like, Happy Birthday Skater Dude

The sport eventually became so popular that a "Go Skateboarding Day" was officially named in 2004. It's celebrated each year on June 21st . . . totally rad!

TAGLINE: Boards for, like, bored surfers

PREDECESSOR: Like . . . not

LESSON: Offer alternatives to existing fads.

Dudes, even though nobody, like, for sure knows who that one stoked guy was who totally got the skateboard thing going, it's like a pretty solid guess it went down like this . . .

> **California Surfer Dude #1:** Bummer dude. There's totally no swells today.
>
> **California Surfer Dude #2:** Major bummer dude. It's completely glassed over.
>
> **California Surfer Dude #1:** You know what'd be an extra-gnarly alternative, bro?
>
> **California Surfer Dude #2:** Sticking some roller skate wheels to a board and going down a major hill?
>
> **California Surfer Dude #1:** Uh, I was gonna say get high, but that totally works, man.
>
> **California Surfer Dude #2:** Stellar. But let's get high first.

Okay, so maybe that's not *exactly* the way things went, but you get the picture.

The first skateboards were sold in Los Angeles at a surf shop, as a nonaquatic activity for California surfers. It began as the brainchild of Bill Richard, owner of the Val Surf Shop, who struck a deal with the Chicago Roller Skate Company to provide wheels for Richard's boards. And thus, "sidewalk surfing," as it was originally called, was born.

90 | ROLLER SKATES

TAGLINE: Dangerous shoes

PREDECESSOR: Just walkin' around

LESSON: People love stuff on wheels, don't they?

Remember the opening credits to *Three's Company* when that hot roller-skater chick would zip past Jack Tripper, getting him excited and making him fall off his bike? Man, that was funny. But what does it have to do with roller skates? Plenty. See, it was placement like that in television and movies that made roller skates a must-have in the '70s and '80s.

This was the time when roller-skating was in its prime. Kids skated in the streets and adults strutted their stuff at roller discos. Then came Scott Olson and his Rollerblades . . . but that's another story.

Roller-skating has its roots in the land of clogs and windmills—the Netherlands. Maybe you already know this about the Dutch, but, apparently, those dike-building, sons-of-guns *loved* to ice-skate. So an unknown Dutch guy in the 1700s set out to make ice-skating a year-round activity. But without the technology to build an indoor rink, he had to settle on skates with wheels instead of blades. Early pairs were made by attaching wooden spools to wooden planks and tying those to people's shoes. The Dutch also love their wooden footwear—see the clog—so the roller skate was an instant success.

However, that unknown Dutch guy didn't bother to patent his invention, and the first roller-skate patent was issued to a Frenchman instead. In 1819, Monsieur Petibledin was recognized for his creation of a roller skate that had two to four wheels aligned at the center of a plank worn on the bottom of the foot. What do you know? It looks like the first *roller skate* was actually the *rollerblade*.

Fiction Is Stranger Than Truth

Just as Dorothy Levitt wrote about the rearview mirror before it was invented, there have been many other inventions that appeared as fiction before they debuted in reality. A few of the more notable ones . . .

- The nuclear submarine (1955): first appeared as the Nautilus in Jules Verne's *Twenty Thousand Leagues Under the Sea* (1870)
- Robotics (1961): first appeared in Isaac Asimov's short story "Runaround" (1942)
- The moon landing (1969): first occurred in Jules Verne's *From the Earth to the Moon* (1865)
- The cell phone (1996): first appeared as the communicator in Gene Roddenberry's *Star Trek* (1966)

91 | REARVIEW MIRROR

TAGLINE: A little makeup mirror in your car—*don't laugh, read on*

PREDECESSOR: Hoping for the best when you changed lanes

LESSON: A lady is always prepared.

Now that talking on a cell phone and texting while driving is illegal in most states, it's kind of ironic to think about how the rearview mirror came to be.

The rearview mirror was first recommended by an early publication. *Car and Driver?* No. *Hotrod Magazine?* No. A 1906 book titled *The Woman and the Car?* Yup.

This forward-thinking, rear-looking publication was authored by Dorothy Levitt, who instructed female drivers to "carry a little hand-mirror in a convenient place when driving" in order to "hold the mirror aloft from time to time in order to see behind while driving in traffic."

The earliest rearview mirror that was mounted on a car rather than held daintily in one's white-gloved hand was kind of a big deal as it was affixed to Ray Harroun's racecar for the first Indianapolis 500 in 1911. But the speedster didn't point to *The Woman and the Car* as the inspiration. Instead, he said the idea came from a similar invention that was used on horse-drawn carts at the time.

The invention wasn't officially introduced until 1914, when auto-manufacturers began installing them. And the person who took credit for their creation wasn't Harroun or Levitt, but Elmer Berger, recognized as being the first person to note the need to install the rearview mirror during manufacturing.

So in hindsight, it seems like quite a few people can claim credit for the invention. I'm not surprised though. Often, objects in people's memories seem clearer than they appear.

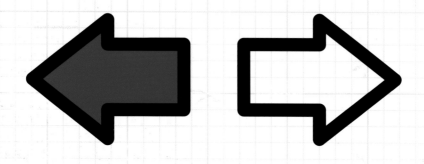

Buick was the first car manufacturer to feature the directional in its automobiles.

92 ELECTRIC TURN SIGNAL

TAGLINE: An indicator light used by conscientious drivers

PREDECESSOR: Sticking your hand out the window

LESSON: Remember to think and blink.

Blinker, directional, turn signal—call it what you may, this important auto feature is another case of optional going standard for safety. While first introduced in 1920 by the Protex Safety Signal Company, inventor C. H. Thomas claims some credit for its creation because of a *Popular Mechanics* article he wrote in 1916 that described a device consisting of a battery-run light bulb connected to a glove. Thomas's lit-up design was meant to help drivers at night, when the cars behind them couldn't see their hands sticking out their windows to signal a turn.

Buick was the first car manufacturer to feature the directional in its automobiles. Their 1938 models came with a flashing turn signal on the rear of the car. And then in 1940, the blinker was also placed at the front, to help with those tricky left hand turns across traffic.

Old School Blinkers

Back before turn signals (and brake lights) became standard, drivers had to use hand signals. You probably learned (and forgot) these in Driver's Ed. So here's a refresher:

- Straight out: left turn
- Elbow bent, hand up: right turn
- Elbow bent, hand down: stop
- Elbow bent, middle finger up: get off my ass

93 VELCRO

TAGLINE: Shockingly loud, tiny hooks and loops

PREDECESSOR: Burrs

LESSON: Mother Nature is a clever Mother %*#!-er.

One summer day in the late 1940s an amateur-mountaineer named George de Mestral took his dog for a walk in the woods. He and his K-9 companion came back covered in those prickly little seed carriers known as burrs. As a part-time inventor, de Mestral was intrigued and inspected one of the annoying things. He saw that the carriers were covered in tiny little hooks that allowed them to cling to things like his dog's fur and his pants' thread. Upon making this observation, de Mestral thrust his face skyward, as lightning struck, illuminating his laboratory in pale blue light, and screamed, "*It's alive!*"* He then set to work designing a two-sided fastener.

One side consisted of stiff, burr-like hooks. The opposite side consisted of loops, much like the threads of his pants. He called this invention "Velcro," combining the words velour and crochet. "It will rival the zipper in its ability to fasten," he announced . . . presumably to his dog.

Patenting the invention in 1955, de Mestal partnered with a French weaver in order to hone his Velcro fastener. De Mestral soon was selling over sixty million yards of Velcro per year, creating a multi*billion*-dollar industry.

So, the next time something inadvertently sticks to you, give it some thought. Maybe there's something you can do with that dog crap on your shoe. I don't know. I'm just saying.

* I made that part up where he acts like an evil scientist. Just wanted to see if you were paying attention.

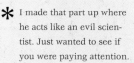

94 STERILE MEDICAL PROCEDURES

TAGLINE: Washing one's hands before shoving them into someone else's body

PREDECESSOR: Killing people

LESSON: Scrub up, pup.

It's amazing what we take for granted these days. We should remember that it wasn't so long ago when performing medical procedures and operations in a sterile medical environment was barely a consideration. In the early nineteenth century, surgeons operated in the clothes they wore to work that day, not even bothering to necessarily put on a lab jacket or apron, let alone a mask. In many cases, butchers were more conscious of being sterile. And the surgical dressings they used on their patient's wounds were made of uncleaned cotton swept from textile mill floors.

Not shockingly, post-surgical mortality in the 1800s was as high as 90 percent due, mostly, to these unsterile conditions. What makes this statistic even more shocking is that all you have to do in order to sterilize a medical instrument is drop it into a pot of boiling water. So why didn't they do that? Why indeed. It was simply because someone, like you, just didn't think of it.

Inspired by Dr. Joseph Lister, who linked operating room infection to germs, Johnson & Johnson was the first company to develop antiseptic wound dressings. This breakthrough was the beginning of an age that sought to improve patient care through the use of sterilization and disinfection technologies. Since then things have improved dramatically in this area and pre-surgical sterilization has became a standard during all medical procedures, saving countless lives.

DID YOU KNOW?

In 1952, Albert Einstein was offered the presidency of the newly formed state of Israel. He declined.

95 GRAVITY

TAGLINE: The theory that we don't float

PREDECESSOR: Sticking to the ground without giving it much thought

LESSON: Observe the world that's right beneath your feet.

Here's a discovery that's not terribly complicated. It goes like this: Newton said we stick to the ground. Einstein said we are pushed to the ground. Either way, we don't sail into space. And it's all thanks to gravity.*

While you might be quick to think Newton's the "Gravity Guy," you'd be mistaken. The theory behind this principle started to formulate in the mind of Greek philosopher Claudius Ptolemy in the second century. The next notable stab at it was by Nicolas Copernicus in the early 1500s. By the late 1500s the theory (not yet called, gravity) really began to gain traction when people started to notice Galileo Galilei's balls. Galileo was showing everybody his balls. And why not? They were magnificent and he was doing exceptional things with them. The Italian scientist started his theorizing when he dropped his balls from the Tower of Pisa. His study of falling bodies and objects rolling down inclines paved the way for Newton and his apples.

I Can See Uranus

Newton's theory made its biggest splash when it helped to prove the existence of Neptune based on the motions of Uranus.

It is rumored that Newton discovered gravity when an apple fell from a tree and struck him in the head. While there are actual accounts of Newton mentioning a falling apple when he was formulating his theory, the fruit did not actually strike the scientist. He merely used it as an example when describing his findings.

 Yes, I am oversimplifying. But if you want an extensive study of the theories of gravity, pick up a real textbook. Try *Gravity from the Ground Up* by Bernard Schutz.

IN 1929, SAM FOSTER SOLD
THE FIRST PAIR OF CIVILIAN
SHADES ON ATLANTIC CITY'S
FAMOUS BOARDWALK.

96 SUNGLASSES

TAGLINE: Glasses you can't really see through

PREDECESSOR: Squinting

LESSON: Make people more comfortable.

The first sunglasses appeared centuries ago when Chinese judges wore smoke-colored lenses to conceal their eyes during trials. They said it was to prevent people in the court from seeing their expressions during trials. (I think they were just trying to look cool.)

From there, James Ayscough picked up the concept of tinting lenses in the eighteenth century. Though these "sunglasses" weren't created as a fashion statement either. Instead, Ayscough believed blue- and green-tinted glass could help correct the eyesight of people with certain vision impairments.

The popularity of sunglasses designed to specifically shade the eye from the sun is really a twentieth-century phenomenon first introduced by the American military. To early military pilots, it was a necessity. The glare from the sun while on flights above cloud-level was extreme and could be the difference between life and death during a dogfight. Thus: Aviator sunglasses were born.

It took some time and a little Atlantic City magic for sunglasses to go from military to mainstream. In 1929, Sam Foster sold the first pair of civilian shades on the coastal getaway's famous boardwalk. It didn't take long for them to become all the rage. By 1930, they were the must-have accessory for a sunny day and remain so to this day.

97 BOWLING

TAGLINE: A sport you can play drunk

PREDECESSOR: Just getting drunk

LESSON: You can make a game out of practically anything.

Bowling. A little like bocce, a bit like horseshoes, sorta like golf, and a lot like rolling a rock at a bunch of sticks. Once again, boredom gives birth to sport.

The roots of the game date way back. The International Bowling Museum and Hall of Fame claims the concept goes all the way back to 5200 B.C. Now that's impressive. No, not the fact that the game can be traced back that far—the fact that there's an International Bowling Museum and Hall of Fame. Though, being able to write that artifacts of the game were found in an ancient Egyptian tomb *is* pretty cool.

Also cool? Using the sport to determine just how sinful you've been. Apparently, German believers would roll a ball at a pin to test their faithfulness and morality. Puts a new spin on the term "holy roller."

Another similarity to the other sports included herein—and a testament to just how entertaining the activity is—the game began to be outlawed in fourteenth-century England. Like the Scots with their golfing, it seems Englishmen were ignoring their archery practice in order to bowl. And that was a big no-no, as archery practice was a national mandate for all men over the age of thirteen during the Hundred Years' War.

But don't think Europeans were the only ones who hated bowling. In 1841, the state of Connecticut banned the sport because it promoted gambling.

I'll bet you it did.

DID YOU KNOW ?

Checkers are known
as draughts in Great
Britain.

98 | CHECKERS

TAGLINE: The lazy-man's chess

PREDECESSOR: Sitting at a card table, staring at one another

LESSON: It's good to be kinged.

Checkers are known as draughts in Great Britain. Those British always have ridiculous names for things. I mean "checkers" makes sense with the whole checkered board thing. But I guess the British have their reasons, and, frankly, they probably named it before we did. In fact, the game's so old, it's had a number of names before both draughts and checkers. Let's take it to the timeline . . .

- 3000 B.C.: People faced off in the earliest form of checkers in Ur, Iraq.
- 1400 B.C.: Always early to the party, the ancient Egyptians played a game with a checkers-like concept.
- A.D. 900: A game called Alquerque is being played on a 5" x 5" board with similar rules.
- 1100: The French start using a chessboard and twelve pieces per player; they come up with all sorts of foo-foo French names like *fierges*, *ferses*, *jeu force*, and *le jeu plaisant de dames*.
- 1700: British draughts are popularized and recorded by a Samuel Johnson foreword to a William Payne book.

And so the basic concept of modern checkers was established.

Today, checkers remains an extremely popular game. Of course, like everything else, it's now often played on computers against an opponent on the Internet. Damn kids today with their computer checkers and rock 'n roll music.

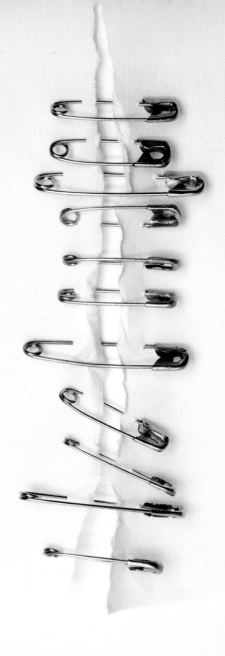

99 SAFETY PIN

TAGLINE: Fastening device, punk rock nose ring, or trailer park broach—your call

PREDECESSOR: The anarchy that was life without the "regular" pin

LESSON: Safety first.

The story behind the safety pin is—wait for it—*fasten*ating. (Sometimes I just can't help myself.)

Anyway, what's so "safe" about a safety pin? It's a giant needle with a clasp on one side. It's not safe. It's a weapon. In fact, according to ancient historian Herodotus of Greece, a group of angry women once used their safety pins to stab an Athenian soldier to death. Gives a whole new meaning to needling a guy, huh?

But the theory behind the name is that it is safer than the straight pin because when you close the clasp, the point of the pin is covered and unable to injure anyone. However, while the poke-free fastener was a less harmful alternative to the straight pin, it was expensive to produce and therefore seen as a luxury only available to the rich. That is until a Quaker found himself in a jam.

In 1849, Walter Hunt, a New York Quaker, was in a load of debt, to the tune of $15. The story goes that he decided to solve this problem by inventing something. On the day before his debt was due, he conceived of a pin that "would not prick the user." Hence the safety pin was born. He sold the invention's patent to the man who held the debt for $400. So he never saw a penny more after that.

THE RIGHTS TO "HAPPY BIRTHDAY TO YOU" WERE BOUGHT IN 1988 FOR $25,000,000.

100 "HAPPY BIRTHDAY TO YOU"

TAGLINE: A silly little song that everyone sings

PREDECESSOR: Not embarrassing the birthday celebrant

LESSON: Write a catchy tune.

This one just boggles the mind.

Ever watch a television show or movie that has a birthday party scene and notice something missing? There's the cake and balloons and even sometimes a little Pin the Tail on the Donkey, but usually they never actually sing "Happy Birthday." (Watch for it next time; they'll usually use "For He's a Jolly Good Fellow" instead.) Why? Well as it turns out, every time the melody and lyrics are used in a broadcast, royalties must be paid to Warner Communications. That's right. Someone makes money off of that little ditty.

The company bought the rights to the song from Burch Tree Group, Ltd. in 1988 for . . . $25 million! Crazy. Especially when you consider that the melody was originally crafted as a morning sing-along for school children.

As it turns out, "Happy Birthday to You" started as "Good Morning to All" in 1859. Written by schoolteacher Mildred J. Hill, the classroom greeting switched its lyrics to celebrate growing a year older in 1893. It wasn't copyrighted until 1935. Although it's used conservatively, the song still reportedly generates $2 million per year in royalties. And it takes the cake as the most popular song in the English-speaking world.

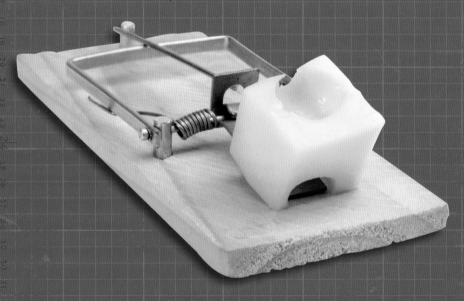

ATKINSON'S MOUSETRAP SLAMS SHUT
IN 38,000THS OF A SECOND.

101 MOUSETRAP

TAGLINE: Cute, little, rodent-crushing device

PREDECESSOR: More mice with fewer spinal injuries

LESSON: Your idea already exists? Build a better one.

In 1897, British inventor James Henry Atkinson designed what we've come to know as the common mousetrap. But that's not to say that people didn't try to trap mice before 1897. There were all kinds of trap contraptions that existed before (and after) Atkinson's—they just weren't as good at catching mice. And while there are literally *thousands* of varieties (and one adorable board game), his version remains the most popular.

Atkinson's design is the one that sits on a little plank of wood and has a spring-loaded, catapult-type mechanism. A piece of food is placed on the trap and when the mouse goes to get it, he triggers the release of a metal bar, which hopefully (but not always) kills the mouse. Atkinson called it the Little Nipper. *Awww!* It sounds so cute. Don't be fooled though—it's a killing machine. The Little Nipper slams shut in 38,000ths of a second, usually crushing the mouse's spine upon impact.

Atkinson sold the patent for his mousetrap to Procter in 1913 for £1,000. (Dummy.) The Procter company has been manufacturing—and making money from—his Little Nipper ever since. Atkinson's mouse exterminator is so successful that Procter has erected a 150-exhibit mousetrap museum in its factory.

All told, the Atkinson mousetrap is the winner among many, as over 4,400 patents have been issued for various types of mousetraps. And only twenty have made money—which leads us full circle back to Ralph Waldo Emerson's remark . . .

> "Build a better mousetrap, and the world will beat a path to your door."

I can't think of a better way to sum up the spirit of this book.
Thanks Ralph!

RESOURCES USED

American Inventors
www.american-inventor.com

Discovery Channel
www.dsc.discovery.com

EduMedia
www.edumedia-sciences.com

Famous Black Inventors
www.black-inventor.com

Famous Women Inventors
www.women-inventors.com

Invention Connection
www.inventionconnection.com

Inventions—Inventors and Inventions—
Famous Inventors
www.topinventionsinfo.com

Inventorprise Inc.
www.inventorprise.com

Inventors Digest
www.inventorsdigest.com

Science
www.sciencemag.org

United Inventors Association (UIA)
www.uiausa.com

United States Patent and
Trademark Office (USPTO)
www.uspto.gov

Wikipedia
www.wikipedia.org

Wise Geek
www.wisegeek.com

APPENDIX A: RESOURCES FOR THE AT-HOME INVENTOR

To Inspire

Check out these sites to see if your idea already exists, or just for inspiration.

Advertising Age
www.adage.com

Alexa
www.alexa.com

Good Ideas Salons
www.goodideassalons.com

Google Trends Labs
www.google.com/trends

Inventors Digest
www.inventorsdigest.com

Kuukan.com
www.kuukan.com

Popular Science
www.popsci.com

Springwise
www.springwise.com

Squidoo
www.squidoo.com

Trendwatch
www.trendwatching.com

Why Not
www.whynot.net

To Educate

Have a great idea, but don't know the next step? Check out these websites to get on the right path.

The Academy of Applied Science
www.aas-world.org

Ask the Inventors!
www.asktheinventors.com

Delphion
www.delphion.com

International Federation of Inventors' Associations
www.invention-ifia.ch

Inventors HQ
www.inventorshq.com

InventorEd
www.inventored.org

Patent Café
www.patentcafe.com

United Inventors Association
www.uiausa.org

United States Patent and Trademark Office
www.uspto.gov

INDEX

ART CREDITS

post-its © istockphoto/BookMama

barbed wire © istockphoto

golf © 2009 Jupiterimages Corporation

crocs © istockphoto/clovercity

condoms © istockphoto/pederk

duct tape background
   © istockphoto/sumnersgraphicsinc

duct tape roll © istockphoto/Hogie

guillotine © 2009 Jupiterimages Corporation

heimlich © istockphoto/apatrimonio

popsicle © istockphoto/ktphotog

bra © istockphoto/wuka

can opener © istockphoto/Devonyu

hula hoop © istockphoto/A-Digit

necktie © istockphoto/AndyL

paper towel © istockphoto/WynnPhoto

band-aid © istockphoto/Nic_Taylor

toilet © istockphoto/Thirteen-Fifty

toilet © Neubau Welt

toothpicks © istockphoto/futureimage

porcupine © 2009 Jupiterimages Corporation

paper clip © istockphoto/AndrewJohnson

stone wheel © istockphoto/jgroup

hamster wheel © istockphoto/ohiophoto

bikini © Comstock, Inc.

turducken © istockphoto/Ace_Create

q-tip © istockphoto/StuartDuncanSmith

ear © 2009 Jupiterimages Corporation

french fries © istockphoto/Alst

dry cleaning © istockphoto/bonniej

pet rock © istockphoto/R_Koopmans

rubber band © istockphoto/bradleym

frisbee © 2009 Jupiterimages Corporation

pencil © istockphoto/mattjeacock

pencil © 2009 Jupiterimages Corporation

candy dots © istockphoto/AuroraMarie

jacks © istockphoto/mguntow

crayons © istockphoto/spfoto

automobile cup holder © 2009 Jupiterimages
   Corporation

soccer © Neubau Welt

paper cup © istockphoto/lishenjun

mannequin © istockphoto/alrax

candy bar © istockphoto/joxxxxjo

bottled water © istockphoto/sampsyseeds

pooper scooper © istockphoto/upheaval

fire © 2009 Jupiterimages Corporation

sliced bread © istockphoto/alejandrophotography

bracelet © istockphoto/Graffizone

drum © 2009 Jupiterimages Corporation

snare drum © Neubau Welt

straws © istockphoto/QUAYSIDE

fishing rod © Neubau Welt

liberty bell © 2009 Jupiterimages Corporation

super balls © istockphoto/NickyBlade

masking tape © istockphoto/PhotographerOlympus

thumbtack © istockphoto/gremlin

tambourine © 2009 Jupiterimages Corporation

plastic milk crate © istockphoto/jzablowski

paper bag © istockphoto/michael1959

punch card © istockphoto/claudiodivizia

shopping cart © Neubau Welt

ART CREDITS

pillow © istockphoto/karammiri

yo-yo © istockphoto/DOConnell

zipper © istockphoto/Auris

horseshoe © 2009 Jupiterimages Corporation

horseshoes © 2009 Jupiterimages Corporation

seatbelt © istockphoto/fstop123

spear © istockphoto/redmal

knife © istockphoto/danesteffes

tractor © 2009 Jupiterimages Corporation

corn © istockphoto/EEI_Tony

lightning rod © 2009 Jupiterimages Corporation

see-saw © istockphoto/AskinTulayOver

pulley © istockphoto/sefaoncul

match box © istockphoto/Gewitterkind

match © istockphoto/arakonyunus

radiator © istockphoto/samposnick

radiator sillhouette © Neubau Welt

fingerprinting © istockphoto/scolzz

pasteurization © istockphoto/narvikk

assembly line © 2009 Jupiterimages Corporation

traffic light © istockphoto/blackred

evolution © istockphoto/Xrisca30

toilet paper © istockphoto/Wwing

shoelace © istockphoto/mcerovac

standardized time © istockphoto/blackred

road sign © istockphoto/clintscholz

sign © Neubau Welt

mass production © 2009 Jupiterimages Corporation

red chair © istockphoto/lleximage

recycling bin © istockphoto/pryzmat

bottling © istockphoto/tmajewski

windshield © istockphoto/mammamaart

old-fashioned wiper © 2009 Jupiterimages
    Corporation

windshield wiper © istockphoto/555DIGIT

skateboard © istockphoto/dave9296

roller skates © istockphoto/klikk

rearview mirror © istockphoto/davidp

burrs © istockphoto/ideeone

hand washing © istockphoto/otisabi

medical tools © Neubau Welt

freefalling © istockphoto/4x6

sunglasses © istockphoto/robnroll

bowling © 2009 Jupiterimages Corporation

checkers © istockphoto/ManuelH

saftey pins © istockphoto/mattjeacock

cake © istockphoto/egal

mousetrap © istockphoto/agencyby

All other images by Elisabeth Lariviere.

ABOUT THE AUTHOR

Anthony Rubino Jr. was born in New Jersey to a first-generation, Italian-American, family. Needless to say he developed a sense of humor at an early age . . . and then felt guilty about it. Channeling that early confusion, he now combines humor, art, and pop culture to create drivel of the highest quality.

Never a stickler for math, Tony wrote five books for his *Life Lesson* "trilogy": *Life Lessons from Your Dog*, *Life Lessons from Your Cat*, *Life Lessons from Elvis*, *Life Lessons from the Bradys*, and *Life Lessons from Melrose Place*. Before that he displayed his steely work ethic by penning, *1001 Reasons to Procrastinate*. And his fear of the discomfort of eternal damnation is reflected in his *The Get Into Heaven Deck: Or Your Money Back*.

Along the way Tony has contributed his articles and cartoons to publications such as: *MAD Magazine*, *Cracked*, *National Lampoon*, the *Chicago Tribune*, and *Opium Magazine*.

He is currently writing the daily cartoon strip, "Daddy's Home" which appears in more than 250 newspapers and websites (*www.daddyshomepage.com*).

When not working on his writing and art in New York City, he spends his time not working on his writing and art in New York City.

Visit *www.rubinocreative.com* for more information and big, big fun.